150 Slow Cooker Steak and Chop Recipes

(150 Slow Cooker Steak and Chop Recipes - Volume 1)

Stacey Doe

Content

150 Awesome Slow Cooker Steak And Chop Recipes

***

1. AUTUMN PORK CHOPS Recipe

Serving: 6 | Prep: | Cook: 480mins | Ready in:

Ingredients

- 6 thick(1") pork chops
- 2 medium acorn squash
- 3/4 tsp. salt
- 2 TBS. butter
- 3/4 cup brown sugar
- 3/4 tsp. Kitchen Bouquet
- 1 TBS. orange juice
- 1/2 tsp. orange peel,greted

Direction

- Cut each squash into 4-5 crossways slices: remove seeds.
- Place 3 chops on bottom of crock-pot.
- Place all squash slices on top of chops
- Then layer the last 3 chops on top
- Combine salt, butter, sugar, bouquet sauce, orange juice and peel
- Spoon over chops
- Cover and cook on low for 6-8 hours
- Serve 2-3 slices of squash with each chop

2. Adele Flank Steak Recipe

Serving: 4 | Prep: | Cook: 480mins | Ready in:

Ingredients

- 1 large white onion chopped
- 1-1/2 pounds flank steak
- 1 large carrot chopped
- 3 teaspoons chili powder
- 1 large green pepper chopped
- 1/2 cup flour
- 2 large tomatoes chopped
- 1-1/2 teaspoons salt
- 1/4 cup red wine
- 1/2 teaspoon pepper
- 1 hot chili pepper seeded
- 3 tablespoons vegetable oil

Direction

- Score steak and rub with chili powder.
- Coat with a mixture of flour, 1/2-teaspoon salt and 1/4 teaspoon seasoned pepper.
- Pound steak on both sides with a wooden mallet to tenderize then cut into 6 pieces.
- Brown steak in hot oil in a large skillet then remove and reserve.
- Sauté onion, carrot, pepper and tomato in pan drippings then add remaining salt and pepper.
- Remove from heat then combine steak and sautéed vegetables in crock pot.
- Add wine and hot chili pepper the cover and cook on low for 8 hours.

3. Apple Pork Chops Recipe

Serving: 6 | Prep: | Cook: 480mins | Ready in:

Ingredients

- 1 onion- sliced
- 6 (1/2 inch thick) pork chops

- 3 apples- peeled, cored and sliced
- 6 TBSP brown sugar
- 1 1/2 TBSP dry mustard
- 1/2 tsp ground cloves
- 3/4 cup of apple juice
- 1 cup chunky apple sauce
- salt and pepper to taste
- butter to saute

Direction

- Sauté onion and apples in butter then place in crock pot.
- Add pork chops to crock pot.
- Pour the apple sauce, spices and apple juice on top.
- Cook on Low for 8-10 hours.

4. Apricot Glazed Pork Chops Recipe

Serving: 4 | Prep: | Cook: 32mins | Ready in:

Ingredients

- nonstick cooking spray
- 1/3 cup reduced-sodium soy sauce
- 1/2 cup apricot whole-fruit preserves
- 2 garlic cloves, minced
- 3 tablespoons ketchup
- 4 pork-loin chops, 1 inch or thicker, preferably bone-in (It's more important that chops be at least 1 inch thick than a particular weight.)

Direction

- Spray inside the slow cooker with non-stick spray. In a small bowl, blend soy sauce, apricot preserves, garlic and ketchup.
- Blot pork chops with paper towels, brush each side with sauce, and place in the slow cooker. If chops must stack in more than one layer to fit, coat first layer with additional sauce before adding remaining chops. Pour all remaining sauce over chops.

- Cover and cook on low until meat is fork-tender, 6 to 8 hours. Remove from the pot and serve.
- PER SERVING: 288 calories; 28 g protein; 26 g carbohydrates; 0 fibre; 7 g fat (3 g saturated); 74 mg cholesterol; 847 mg sodium. The nutritional analysis is based on 6-ounce servings.

5. Asian Crockpot Steak Recipe

Serving: 4 | Prep: | Cook: 10hours | Ready in:

Ingredients

- 1/2 tablespoon olive oil
- 1 pound beef round, cut into stir fry strips
- 1/4 cup onion, chopped
- 1 garlic clove, minced
- 1 cup of bok choy, sliced or shredded
- 1 1/2 cups beef broth
- 1/4 cup soy sauce
- 1/2 teaspoon ground ginger
- 1 1/2 tablespoons cornstarch mixed in 1/2 cup cold water
- 2 cups broccoli, cooked

Direction

- Sauté meat in oil. Put in crockpot.
- Add other ingredients except cornstarch and broccoli. Cover and cook on low for 10 hours.
- Pour meat and sauce into pot, bring to a boil and add thickener.
- Stir in cooked broccoli and serve.

6. Asian Pepper Steak Recipe

Serving: 8 | Prep: | Cook: 240mins | Ready in:

Ingredients

- 3 lbs beef sirloin

- 3 Tbs cornstarch,for dusting meat
- 3 cloves garlic,grated or finely chopped
- 2 Tbs ginger,grated
- 1 large onion,sliced
- 3 red bell peppers,sliced
- 3 yellow bell peppers,sliced
- 1 8 oz. can tomato sauce
- 4 Tbs brown sugar
- 3/4 c soy sauce
- ground black pepper to taste
- 2 c rice
- Topper:
- 2 c bean sprouts
- 1 c cilantro ,roughly chopped
- 2 limes
- chopped scallions

Direction

- In large skillet, sear the meat in some olive oil until nice and brown both sides. Remove steak to cutting board and slice into 1" strips
- Place sliced steak into crock pot bowl, then dust the meat with cornstarch and mix the meat around till there is no visible cornstarch.
- Add remaining ingredients except for topper ingredients to crock pot, cover and cook high for 4 hours or low for 6 hours.
- When ready to serve, get med bowl, mix topper ingredients and place portion of mixture on top of each portion, if desired. This adds a pop of freshness and texture. Serve over rice.

7.   BBQ Beef On A Bun Recipe

Serving: 8 | Prep: | Cook: 480mins | Ready in:

Ingredients

- 3 Lb bonless sirloin roast
- 1 ½ Cup ketchup
- ¼ Cup packed brown sugar
- 2 Tbsp mustard
- 2 Tbsp worchester sauce

- 1 tsp liquid smoke
- ½ tsp salt
- ¼ tsp black pepper
- ¼ tsp garlic powder

Direction

- -Put Roast in slow cooker
- -Combine ingredients and pour over roast
- -Cook 8-10 hours on low, or 4-5 hours on high
- -When done, pull out and shred with a fork
- -Return shredded roast to sauce
- -spoon onto sandwich buns
- Enjoy!

8.   Bar B Qd Pork Steaks Crockpot Recipe

Serving: 6 | Prep: | Cook: 480mins | Ready in:

Ingredients

- 6 pork steaks OR Chops
- 1 ts Fat
- 1 1/2 c ketchup
- 1 1/2 c water
- 1/4 c vinegar
- 1/4 c worcestershire sauce
- 2 ts salt
- 2 ts chili powder
- 2 ts paprika
- 1 ts pepper
- 1/2 ts Accent
- 2 lg Onions; sliced very thin
- 1 ts salt
- 1 ts Accent
- 1/4 ts pepper

Direction

- Use a 5 qt. crockpot. Place fat in crockpot and melt on HIGH. Add meat and turn to coat with fat. Season meat with mixture of last 3 ingredients. Add all other ingredients. Cook on LOW for 8-9 hrs.

9. Beef And Button Mushroom Stroganoff Recipe

Serving: 6 | Prep: | Cook: 8hours20mins | Ready in:

Ingredients

- 3 pounds boneless sirloin or beef round steak, cut into thin strips
- 1/2 cup flour
- 2 teaspoons salt
- 1 teaspoon freshly ground pepper
- 2 medium onions, thinly sliced into rings
- 20 fresh button mushrooms
- 1 1/2 cups beef broth
- 1/4 cup dry white wine
- 1 teaspoon Worcestershire sauce
- 1 1/2 cups sour cream
- 1/4 cup flour
- 4 cups egg noodles, cooked and drained
- 2 tablespoons fresh parsley, minced

Direction

- Dredge the beef strips in the flour, salt and pepper. Place the coated beef strips in the Crock-Pot® Slow Cooker. Add the onions, mushrooms, beef broth, wine, and Worcestershire sauce.
- Cover; cook on Low 8 to 10 hours (or on High for 4 to 5 hours).
- Before serving, combine the sour cream and flour thoroughly, and add to the stoneware contents. Mix well and let cook for an additional 10 minutes.
- Serve over the egg noodles. Garnish with the parsley.

10. Beef Stroganoff Recipe

Serving: 6 | Prep: | Cook: 90mins | Ready in:

Ingredients

- 1 Pkg. round steak
- 2 T. fat
- 3 onions Chopped
- 2 Jars mushrooms
- 1 Large can tomatoes drained
- 1 T. worcestershire sauce
- 3/4 T. salt
- 1/2 t. pepper
- 2 T. White Vinagar
- 1 Carton Whipping Cread

Direction

- Sprinkle Garlic Salt and Tobasco Sauce over meat. Brown in electric or heavy skillet. Add next 6 ingredients to meat. Cover and simmer over real low heat for 1 1/2 hrs. After 1 hour add 2 T. Vinegar to 1 Carton of Whipping Cream. Let stand at room temperature for 30 minutes. Add to meat mixture. Serve over rice or noodles.

11. Beef Tips And Noodles Recipe

Serving: 4 | Prep: | Cook: 240mins | Ready in:

Ingredients

- 2 to 3 lbs of sirloin or sirloin tip steak, cubed
- 2 tablespoons cooking oil
- 1 pound fresh mushrooms sliced
- 1 tablespoon butter
- 1/4 cup thinly sliced onion
- 1 can cream of onion soup
- 1/4 cup red cooking wine
- 2 tablespoons worcestershire sauce
- 1/4 to 1/2 cup water or beef broth
- noodles cooked according to package directions

Direction

- Heat oil in large skillet.
- Add beef cubes and brown.

- Add onions to meat mixture just before meat is ready to remove and cook until onions are tender.
- Remove meat mixture and place in slow cooker.
- Add butter and mushrooms to skillet and cook over medium heat until soft.
- Add mushrooms to slow cooker.
- Put soup, wine and Worcestershire sauce in skillet and stir to mix.
- Heat and add to slow cooker.
- Stir to mix all ingredients. Add water to desired consistency.
- Cook on low for 4 hours.
- Serve over noodles.

12. Beef Tips In Crockpot Recipe

Serving: 8 | Prep: | Cook: 480mins | Ready in:

Ingredients

- 3 lbs. beef tips (round steak or sirloin)
- 2 Tbsp. olive oil
- 1 can cream of mushroom soup
- 1 can French onion soup (not the dry mix)
- 1 8-oz carton sour cream (fat free works fine)

Direction

- Brown beef tips in olive oil.
- Mix with the two soups in a crockpot.
- Cook on low all day or 6 to 8 hours.
- Just before serving, add the sour cream.
- Serve over rice or egg noodles.
- Note: I like to also serve on rice, wild rice, or a mixture of the two.
- Note: Beef tips are bite size pieces of steak. You can also slice in strips if you prefer.

13. Beef And Broccoli Recipe

Serving: 4 | Prep: | Cook: 15mins | Ready in:

Ingredients

- 3/4 # beef sirloin steak
- 1 Tbsp vegetable oil
- 1 clove garlic
- 1 medium onion, sliced thin
- 1 can cream of broccoli soup
- 1/4 cup water
- 1 Tbsp soy sauce
- 2 cups broccoli flowerets

Direction

- Slice beef across the grain into very thin slices
- Cook beef and garlic until browned
- Add onion and cook 5-10 minutes, stirring often
- Stir in soup, water and soy sauce
- Heat to boiling and add broccoli
- Reduce heat to low
- Cover and simmer for 5-10 minutes or until vegetables are tender
- Note: This can be served over cooked rice, noodles or as is

14. Beef In Mushroom Gravy Recipe

Serving: 6 | Prep: | Cook: 480mins | Ready in:

Ingredients

- 2 to 2 1/2 lbs boneless round steak (I even use stew meat)
- 1 can (10 3/4oz) cream mushroom soup
- 1 to 2 envelopes onion soup mix
- 1/2 Cup water
- mashed potatoes or biscuits

Direction

- Cut steak into serving size portions place in slow cooker. In a medium size bowl combine mushroom soup, soup mix & water, pour over beef.
- Cover & cook on low for 7 to 8 hours or until meat is tender. (Some slow cookers cook differently, mine cooks faster, so cook accordingly to your cooker)
- Serve over mashed potatoes or biscuits if desired.

15. CROCK POT PEPPER STEAK Recipe

Serving: 4 | Prep: | Cook: 300mins | Ready in:

Ingredients

- 1 - 2 lb. round steak, cut into 1 inch pieces
- 1 onion, thinly sliced
- 2 - 3 cloves garlic, minced
- 1 tsp. worcestershire sauce
- 1 can tomato soup
- 1/2 empty soup can filled with water
- 1 green and 1 red pepper, seeded and thinly sliced Place

Direction

- Cut steak, onion, garlic, and Worcestershire sauce into crock pot. Pour in soup and water.
- Cook on high for 1 hour.
- Cook on low for 3 to 4 hours.
- The last hour of cooking, put pepper in.
- Serve over rice or toast.
- For variety, use cream of mushroom soup and a small can of sliced mushrooms.
- Pork chops, cubed pork loin or chicken breasts can be substituted for the steak.
- Serve over steamed rice.

16. CUBE STEAKS WITH GRAVY Recipe

Serving: 6 | Prep: | Cook: 68mins | Ready in:

Ingredients

- 1/3-cup flour
- 6 beef cube steaks
- 1-tablespoon vegetable oil
- 1 large onion, sliced and separated into rings
- 3 cups water, divided
- 1 envelope brown gravy mix
- 1 envelope mushroom gravy mix
- 1 envelope onion gravy mix

Direction

- Place flour in a large resalable plastic bag. Add the steaks a few at a time, and shake until completely coated. In a skillet, cook the steaks in oil until lightly browned on each side. Transfer to a slow cooker. Add the onion and 2 cups water. Cover and cook on low for 8 hours or until meat is tender. In a bowl, whisk together gravy mixes with remaining water. Add to the slow cooker; cook 30 minutes longer. Serve over mashed potatoes or noodles. If the gravy is too thick just add more water.

17. Cherry Porkchops Recipe

Serving: 4 | Prep: | Cook: 45mins | Ready in:

Ingredients

- 1 (21 ounce) can cherry pie filling
- 4 pork chops

Direction

- Pour cherry pie filling into slow cooker.
- Add pork chops and stir to coat with filling.
- Cover and cook on low for 4 to 5 hours.

- Cook until meat is no longer pink inside and thermometer reads 160 to 170 degrees.
- Good served with rice.

18. Chicken Fried Pork Chops Crock Pot Recipe Recipe

Serving: 6 | Prep: | Cook: 480mins | Ready in:

Ingredients

- 1/2 c flour
- 2 tsp salt
- prepared mustard
- 1/2 tsp garlic powder
- 6 pork chops
- 2 tbsps olive oil
- 1 can cream of chicken or cream of celery soup
- 1/3 c water

Direction

- Mix up the flour, salt and garlic powder. Smear mustard on each side of the chops, just enough to cover lightly and then dredge in the dry ingredients. Heat a skillet and add the olive oil. Brown the chops on both sides. This step add the bits of goodness that you'll want in your gravy when it's all done. Put the chops in the crock pot. Mix the soup and water and pour over chops. Cover the crock pot and cook for 4 hours on high or 8 hours on low. Serve with mashed potatoes or rice or noodles. Add the crock pot juice as gravy. Thicken with some flour if needed, but usually it's not required for a nice gravy consistency.

19. Chicken Lickin' Good Pork Chops Recipe

Serving: 4 | Prep: | Cook: 8hours | Ready in:

Ingredients

- 6 to 8 pork chops or pork steaks
- 1 tbsp. salt
- 1/2 tsp. garlic powder
- oil
- 1/2 c. flour
- 1 1/2 tsp. dry mustard
- 1 can cream of chicken soup

Direction

- Mix dry ingredients together; then dredge pork chops in the mixture. Cover bottom of skillet with oil and brown chops. Put browned chops in crock pot. Add can of soup, cover and cook on low for 6 to 8 hours or on high for 3 1/2 hours. Because the soup makes good gravy, 2 cans of soup can be used if you want extra gravy.

20. Chili Pork Chops Recipe

Serving: 68 | Prep: | Cook: 420mins | Ready in:

Ingredients

- 1/2 cup chopped onion
- cooking spray
- 2-3 garlic clove or 1/2t garlic powder
- 2 tablespoons worcestershire sauce
- 1/2 cup water
- 3/4 cup ketchup
- 1-2 teaspoon chili powder
- 6-8 pork chops, trimmed (bone in preferred)
- salt and pepper

Direction

- Cook onions with cooking spray until lightly brown.
- Add garlic, Worcestershire sauce, chili powder, water, ketchup and salt and pepper.
- Cover and simmer the sauce for 10 minutes.
- Arrange pork chops in crock pot, pour sauce over the chops.

- Cover and cook on LOW HEAT for 6-7 hours.

21. Chipotle Beef Recipe

Serving: 6 | Prep: | Cook: 480mins | Ready in:

Ingredients

- 1 1/2 Lb boneless beef round steak or a small roast
- 1 14oz. can of diced tomatoes
- 1 med. red onion, diced
- 2 canned chipotle peppers in adobo sauce, chopped
- 1-2 tsp oregano
- 1 clove minced garlic
- dash of salt
- dash of cumin

Direction

- Trim fat from meat and set in your crock pot with all ingredients.
- Cook on low for 8-10 hours or high for 4-5 hours.
- Remove meat and shred with 2 forks.
- Stir in reserved juices - enough to moisten or make saucy.

22. Citrus Pork Chops Recipe

Serving: 5 | Prep: | Cook: 56mins | Ready in:

Ingredients

- pork chops center cut, family pack
- 1 Can of chopped pineapple (do not drain)
- 1 can of peaches (do not drain)
- 1/4 cup apple cider vinegar
- 1/2 cup brown sugar
- 3 tbsp. honey

Direction

- Combine all ingredients
- Mix well
- Add chops and a little extra water to cover them if the juice does not
- Cook for 2 hours on high, then 3 on medium or until tender

23. Coffee Flavored Beef Roast Recipe

Serving: 8 | Prep: | Cook: 360mins | Ready in:

Ingredients

- 6 medium potatoes,cut in wedges
- 6 medium carrots,cut into 1" lengths
- 2 beef sirloin tip roasts (2 to 3 lbs ea)
- 1 tsp salt,divided
- 1/2 tsp pepper,divided
- 2 tsp canola oil1 medium onion,halved and sliced
- 2 c whole fresh mushrooms,quarterd
- 2 garlic cloves ,minced
- 1-1/2 c brewed coffee
- 1 tsp chili powder
- 3 Tb cornstarch
- 1/4 c cold water

Direction

- Place potatoes and carrots in a 6 qt. slow cooker. Sprinkle beef with half of the salt and pepper. In a large skillet, brown beef in oil on all sides. Transfer to a slow cooker.
- In same skillet, sauté onions in drippings for 2 mins. Add mushrooms and garlic; cook 2 mins longer. Stir in the coffee, chili powder and remaining salt and pepper. Pour over meat. Cover and cook on low for 6 to 8 hours or till meat is tender.
- Remove meat and vegetables to a serving platter; keep warm. Skim fat from cooking juices; transfer to a small saucepan. Bring liquid to a boil. Combine cornstarch and water till smooth; gradually stir into the pan. Bring

to a boil; cook and stir 2 mins or until thickened. Serve with meat and vegetables.

24. Colcannon And Whiskey Steak: Recipe

Serving: 6 | Prep: | Cook: 6hours | Ready in:

Ingredients

- Onion Mirepoix:
- * 2 yellow onions, diced
- * 1 carrot, peeled and minced
- * 1 celery stalk, minced
- * 1 bay leaf
- * fresh ground black pepper
- * 4 tbs. salted butter
- * 1 clove garlic, peeled and minced
- * 1/2 cup of water
- Sautéed Curly kale or Crisp Green Cabbage:
- * 2 tbs. butter
- * onion mirepoix (recipe above)
- * 1 lb. curly kale or crisp green cabbage, shredded
- * ground sea salt (to taste)
- * ground black pepper (to taste)
- * dash of freshly grated nutmeg
- Mashed Potatoes:
- * 5 lbs. potatoes, cut into even pieces
- * salt (to taste)
- * pepper (to taste)
- * 2 cups sour cream or buttermilk
- * 1 stick butter
- Colcannon:
- * mashed potatoes (recipe above)
- * sautéed curly kale or crisp green cabbage (recipe above)
- * scallions – diced
- * bacon bits (optional) for garnish
- whiskey Steak:
- 1/2 cup brown sugar
- 1/2 cup whiskey
- 3 tbs. olive oil
- 1/2 tablespoon garlic powder

- 1/4 cup soy sauce
- 1 tablespoon salt
- 1 tablespoon pepper
- Grass-fed Tri-Tip steak

Direction

- Onion Mirepoix: Place all the ingredients except the water into the slow-cooker. Cover. Cook on low for 3 hours. Add water. Stir. Cover. Cook for 2+ more hours. Remove bay leaf.
- Sautéed Curly Kale or Crisp Green Cabbage:
- Directions: In a large saucepan, lightly sauté the onion mirepoix in the butter until warm and aromatic. Wilt in the curly kale/green cabbage. Cook until tender, but still crisp.
- Mashed Potatoes: Directions: Boil potatoes in salted water until tender. Drain. Add salt, pepper, sour cream (or buttermilk) and butter. Mix or mash until it reaches desired consistency.
- Colcannon:
- Directions: Fold the sautéed crisp green cabbage or curly kale into the mashed potatoes and top with scallions. Optional bacon bits for garnish.
- Whiskey Steak:
- Directions: Warm all the ingredients except the steak together. Place warmed, mixed ingredients in air tight bag with grass-fed tri-tip steak. Massage marinade into steak. Place bag with steak into the refrigerator for 2-6 hours. Remove from plastic, air-tight bag. Grill.

25. Corn Stuffed Pork Chops In The Crock Pot Recipe

Serving: 6 | Prep: | Cook: 480mins | Ready in:

Ingredients

- 6 pork chops 2" thick
- 7 ounce can whole kernel corn

- 1 cup soft bread crumbs
- 1 tablespoon instant minced onion
- 2 tablespoons minced green pepper
- 1 teaspoon salt
- 1/2 teaspoon sage

Direction

- Cut a horizontal slit in side of each chop forming a pocket for stuffing.
- Mix corn with juices, bread crumbs, onion, pepper, salt and sage.
- Spoon corn mixture into slits then close with toothpicks.
- Place on metal rack or trivet in crock pot then cover and cook on low for 8 hours.

26. Creamy Crock Pot Pork Chops Recipe

Serving: 4 | Prep: | Cook: 8mins | Ready in:

Ingredients

- 4-6 pork chops, bone in or boneless
- flour
- salt & pepper to taste
- 1/4 cup oil
- 1 large onion, sliced
- 2 chicken bouillon cubes
- 2 cups hot water
- 8 oz. sour cream

Direction

- Season pork chops to taste with salt and pepper and dredge in flour, Heat oil in a frying pan, lightly brown chops on both sides. Remove from pan and place in slow cooker.
- Top with onion slices.
- Dissolve bouillon in hot water and pour over pork chops.
- Cover and cook on low 7-8 hours.
- After pork chops have cooked, stir 2 Tbsp. flour into sour cream. Stir sour cream into

cooking juices in crock pot. (Not necessary to be totally blended.)
- Turn cooker to high for 15-30 minutes or until liquid is slightly thickened.
- Serve with potatoes, noodles or rice.

27. Creamy Slow Cooker Marsala Pork Recipe

Serving: 6 | Prep: | Cook: 360mins | Ready in:

Ingredients

- 1 cup flour
- 1 tablespoon minced fresh rosemary
- 1 teaspoon dry mustard powder
- 1 teaspoon salt
- 1 teaspoon garlic powder
- 1/2 teaspoon ground black pepper
- 6 (4 ounce) pork chops
- 2 tablespoons vegetable oil
- 1 onion, sliced
- 1 (4 ounce) package sliced mushrooms
- 1 clove garlic, minced
- 1 (10.75 ounce) can condensed cream of mushroom soup
- 1/2 cup marsala wine

Direction

- Stir together the flour, rosemary, mustard, salt, garlic powder, and pepper in a bowl.
- Dredge the pork chops in the seasoned flour, shake off excess, and set aside.
- Heat the vegetable oil in a large skillet over medium-high heat.
- Add the pork chops and cook until golden brown on both sides, about 4 minutes per side.
- Place the onion, mushrooms, and garlic into a slow cooker.
- Add the seared pork chops, then pour in the cream of mushroom soup and Marsala wine.
- Cover, and cook on Low until the chops are tender, 6 to 8 hours.

28. Crock Pot Beef Stroganoff Recipe

Serving: 8 | Prep: | Cook: 480mins | Ready in:

Ingredients

- 3 lb. beef round steak, 1/2 inch thick
- 1/2 c. flour
- 2 tsp. salt
- 1/8 tsp. pepper
- 1/2 tsp. dry mustard
- 2 med. onions, thinly sliced and separated into rings
- 2 8 oz pkgs fresh mushrooms, sliced
- 1 (10 1/2 oz.) can condensed beef broth
- 1/4 c. dry white wine (optional)
- 1 1/2 c. sour cream
- 1/4 c. flour

Direction

- Trim all excess fat from steak
- Cut meat into 3-inch strips about 1/2 inch wide
- Combine 1/2 cup flour, salt, pepper & dry mustard; toss with steak strips to coat thoroughly
- Place coated steak strips in crock pot; stir in onion rings and mushrooms
- Add beef broth and wine; stir well
- Cover and cook on low setting for 8-10 hours
- Before serving, combine sour cream with 1/4 cup flour; stir into crock pot
- Serve stroganoff over rice or noodles.

29. Crock Pot Oklahoma Steak Soup Recipe

Serving: 4 | Prep: | Cook: | Ready in:

Ingredients

- 3 c. water
- 3 sm. chopped onions
- 3 stalks chopped celery
- 2 sliced carrots
- 1 (1 lb.) can tomatoes
- 1 tsp. pepper
- 1 (10 oz.) frozen vegetables
- 1 lb. sirloin steak, cubed
- 2 to 4 tbsp. beef bouillon
- 1/2 c. butter
- 1/2 c. flour

Direction

- Put all except butter and flour into Crockpot. Cook low 8 to 10 hours. 1 1/2 hours before serving, turn up to high. Make roux of butter and flour stirring until smooth. Add to soup to thicken.

30. Crock Pot Pepper Steak Recipe Recipe

Serving: 0 | Prep: | Cook: 9hours | Ready in:

Ingredients

- http://tastyquery.com/recipes-for/crock-pot-meals
- Crock Pot Pepper Steak Recipe
- Ingredients:
- 1 1/2 pounds flank steak thinly sliced
- 1 large onion slices
- 2 bell peppers any color sliced
- 2 tablespoons soy sauce
- 2 tablespoons sesame oil
- 1 tablespoon brown sugar
- 3 cloves garlic sliced
- rice (optional)

Direction

- Directions:

- Spray 3 1/2 qt. crock pot with pam. Put everything in the crock, mix well. Cook on low 8-9 hours.
- Serve over rice if desired (points for rice not included)
- Makes 4 (1 Cup Servings)
- Nutritional Info Per Serving: 269 Calories; 16g Fat; 23g Protein; 7g Carbs; 1g Fibre; 58mg Cholesterol;
- 424mg Sodium

31. Crock Pot Pork Chop Supper Recipe

Serving: 6 | Prep: | Cook: 420mins | Ready in:

Ingredients

- 6 pork loin or rib chops, 1/2" thick
- 6 medium new potatoes (about 1 1/2 lbs) cut into eighths
- 1 can cream of mushroom soup
- 1 can (4 oz.) mushroom stems and pieces, drained
- 2 Tbl white wine
- 1/4 tsp dried thyme leaves
- 1/2 tsp garlic powder
- 1/2 tsp worcestershire sauce
- 3 Tbl glour
- 1Tbl diced pimientos
- 1 pkg (10 oz) frozen green peas, rinsed and drained.

Direction

- Spray a 10" non-stick skillet; heat over medium high heat
- Cook chops in skillet, turning once until brown
- Place potatoes in 3 1/2 to 6 qt. slow cooker
- Whisk together soup, mushrooms, wine, thyme, garlic powder, Worcestershire sauce and flour; spoon half of mixture over potatoes
- Place chops on potatoes; cover with remaining soup mixture.

- Cover and cook on low heat setting 6 to 7 hours or until pork is tender
- Remove pork and keep warm
- Stir pimientos and peas into slow cooker.
- Cover and cook on low about 15 minutes or until peas are tender
- Serve with chops

32. Crock Pot Pork Chops Recipe

Serving: 4 | Prep: | Cook: 480mins | Ready in:

Ingredients

- 4 pork chops, 1/2" thick
- 2 medium onions, chopped
- 2 celery ribs, chopped
- 1 large green pepper, sliced
- 1 (14.5 ounce) can stewed tomatoes
- 1/2 cup ketchup
- 2 tablespoons cider vinegar
- 2 tablespoons brown sugar
- 2 tablespoons worcestershire sauce
- 1 tablespoon lemon juice
- 1 beef bouillon cube
- 2 tablespoons cornstarch
- 2 tablespoons water

Direction

- Salt and pepper chops, if desired.
- Add all ingredients except water and cornstarch to the crock pot.
- Cook on low setting for 5 1/2 hours.
- Mix cornstarch and water together and stir into crock pot.
- Cook 30 minutes more.
- Serve over rice.

33. Crock Pot Pork Chops Recipe

Serving: 5 | Prep: | Cook: 5mins | Ready in:

Ingredients

- 5 boneless pork chops
- 1 Family size can of cream of mushroom soup
- 1 box of Lipton Onion Soup Mix (it has two packets inside)
- 1 16 oz. of sour cream
- small can of sliced mushrooms
- 3/4 can of water
- 2 TBSP butter or margarine
- garlic powder (your taste preference)
- pepper Dash

Direction

- Dash garlic powder and pepper on the Pork chops
- Put the butter or margarine in a skillet and lightly brown the chops
- In a bowl mix Soup, soup mixes, Sour cream and mushrooms set aside
- Put chops in bottom of crock and put the soup mix on top of them
- Add 3/4 can of water and lightly mix
- Put in your crock on low for 5 hours, or high for 3
- Enjoy!! God Bless :)

---

34. Crock Pot Pulled Pork And Coleslaw Sandwiches Recipe

Serving: 8 | Prep: | Cook: 9mins | Ready in:

Ingredients

- Pulled Pork:
- 1/2 cup ketchup
- 1/3 cup cider vinegar
- 1/3 cup packed brown sugar
- 1 (6 oz) can tomato paste
- 2 tablespoons worcestershire sauce
- 2 tablespoons yellow mustard
- 1 1/2 teaspoons salt
- 1 teaspoon onion powder
- 3 lb pork sirloin roast, cut into 3

- Cole slaw:
- 1 bag of coleslaw mix
- 1/2 cup of mayo
- 3 tablespoons canola oil
- 1/4 cup sugar
- 1 tablespoon cider vinegar
- 1/4 teaspoon salt
- 1/2 teaspoon celery seed
- 1 teaspoon onion powder
- 8 sandwich/hamburger buns

Direction

- For the pulled pork: Mix together all ingredients except pork roast in crockpot. Add pork and turn pieces to coat with sauce. Cover, and cook on low for 6-8 hours. Once done, shred pork and stir to completely incorporate in sauce.
- For the coleslaw: Mix all ingredients well in a large bowl. Cover and let chill for 1-2 hours.
- Once pork is done and coleslaw is chilled, make sandwiches! Put some pork on your bun and top with coleslaw. Enjoy!

---

35. Crock Pot Round Steak Recipe

Serving: 4 | Prep: | Cook: 380mins | Ready in:

Ingredients

- 1 large round steak
- 4 large carrots, sliced
- 4 large potatoes, sliced
- 1 can cream of mushroom soup
- 1/2 cup water
- 1 teaspoon lemon pepper
- salt and pepper to taste

Direction

- Cut round steak into serving slices.
- Sprinkle with lemon pepper on both sides.
- Put in crock pot and add other ingredients.
- Let simmer on low for 5 hours.

36. Crock Pot Steak Recipe

Serving: 4 | Prep: | Cook: 8hours | Ready in:

Ingredients

- 1 medium onion, sliced and separated into rings
- 1 small bell pepper, sliced
- 4 oz.. mushrooms, sliced thick
- 2 lb. round steak, cut into 4 pieces
- 1 10 1/4 oz.. can cream of mushroom soup
- 1/4 cup beef broth
- 1/2 tsp. red pepper flakes

Direction

- Put onions, mushrooms and peppers in bottom of crock pot
- In skillet, brown meat on both sides
- Place on top of vegetables
- In mixing bowl, mix broth, soup and red pepper flakes together
- Pour over meat and vegetables
- Cover and cook on Low 6-8 hours, or until meat is tender but not overcooked

37. Crock Pot Swiss Steak Recipe

Serving: 4 | Prep: | Cook: 68mins | Ready in:

Ingredients

- 1 1/2 to 2 pounds round steak
- 2 tablespoons flour
- 1 teaspoon salt
- 1/8 teaspoon pepper
- 2 tablespoons oil
- 1 (16-ounce) can tomatoes, cut up
- 1 large onion, sliced
- 1 green pepper, sliced
- 1 rib celery, thinly sliced

- 1 tablespoon thick bottled steak sauce

Direction

- Cut steak into serving-size pieces. Coat with flour, salt and pepper.
- In large skillet or slow cooking pot with browning unit, brown meat in oil.
- Pour off excess fat.
- In slow cooking pot, combine meat with tomatoes, onion, green pepper, celery and steak sauce.
- Cover pot and cook on low for 6 to 8 hours or until tender.
- Thicken juices with additional flour, dissolved in a small amount of water, if desired.
- Serve with mashed potatoes.

38. Crock Pot Cubed Minute Steak Recipe

Serving: 6 | Prep: | Cook: 360mins | Ready in:

Ingredients

- 5 yukon gold potatoes.
- 4 cubed steaks.
- 1 clove garlic diced.
- 1pkg. mushroom gravy mix.
- 1 1/2 cup water.
- 1 white or red onion quartered and seperated.
- 1 can button mushrooms.
- 1 can cream of mushroom soup, undeluted.

Direction

- Quarter and halve potatoes into bite size pieces.
- Season with salt and pepper.
- Layer Cubed steaks over potatoes and season.
- Add garlic clove diced.
- Spread pkg. of mushroom gravy mix over meat.
- Add water, mushrooms, onions, and soup over top of meat.

- Slow cook on high for 6 hrs. On high.
- The meat has broken down and is so tender.
- This dish is so easy and provides great flavour to a simple and easy meal.

39. Crock Pot Chicken With Black Beans And Cream Cheese Recipe

Serving: 6 | Prep: | Cook: 4hours | Ready in:

Ingredients

- 6-7 1/2 frozen boneless chicken breasts
- 1 (23 1/4 ounce) can of black beans
- 1 (22 1/2 ounce) can sweet corn
- 1 (22 1/2 ounce) jar of salsa
- 1(12 ounce) package of cream cheese

Direction

- 1) Take the frozen chicken breasts and place them in the crock-pot
- 2) Drain you beans and your corn and add to the crock-pot. Add your salsa
- 3) Cover crock-pot until the chicken is well done
- 4) Add one package of cream cheese (just stick it on top!) and let it sit for about half an hour
- 5) ENJOY!!

40. Crock Pot Pork And Gravy Recipe

Serving: 4 | Prep: | Cook: 360mins | Ready in:

Ingredients

- 4-5 pork shoulder chops
- 1 pkg. onion soup mix
- 1 can cream of chicken soup
- 10 oz. water

Direction

- Trim excess fat off chops and cut into stew size pieces
- Lightly brown in skillet and place in the bottom of crock-pot
- Combine remaining ingredients and pour over pork
- Cook 6 hours on low.
- Great when served over garlic mashed potatoes

41. Crockery Pot Fajitas Recipe

Serving: 4 | Prep: | Cook: 360mins | Ready in:

Ingredients

- 1 to 11/2 lbs. boneless beef round steak, cut in strips
- 1/2 lg. red bell pepper, cut in strips
- 1/2 lg. green bell pepper, cut in strips
- 1 lg. onion, cut into thin slices
- 1 pkg. dry fajita mix (1 oz.)
- 1/4 c. water
- 6 lg. flour tortillas
- 2 sm. tomatoes, chopped
- 1 avocado, peeled, thinly sliced
- 1/2 c. dairy sour cream

Direction

- In slow-cooker, combine beef, peppers, onion, fajita mix and water. Cover and cook on LOW 5 to 6 hours or until meat is tender. Warm tortilla in microwave according to pkg. directions. With spoon, lift meat mixture out of pot. Place about 3/4 cup mixture along center of each tortilla. Top with chopped tomato, sour cream and avocado. Fold both sides over filling.

42. Crockpot Beef Stroganoff Recipe

Serving: 6 | Prep: | Cook: 480mins | Ready in:

Ingredients

- 1-1/2 lbs. beef sirloin tip, cut into cubes (I added some seasoning salt to my steak)
- 16 oz. pkg. baby carrots
- can of stem and peices mushrooms or sliced fresh mushrooms (how much you would like)
- 1 onion, chopped
- 3 cloves garlic, minced
- 1/2 tsp. dried oregano leaves
- 1/2 tsp. salt
- 1/2 tsp. dried thyme leaves
- 1/8 tsp. pepper
- 1 bay leaf
- 1-1/2 cups beef broth
- 1/2 cup apple juice
- 8 oz. carton sour cream
- 1/4 cup flour
- 1/4 cup water

Direction

- Combine everything except sour cream, flour, and water in a 3-1/2 quart slow cooker. Cook on low heat for 8-10 hours (high for 4-5 hours). Remove and discard bay leaf.
- Combine sour cream, flour, and water in medium bowl and mix well, using a whisk.
- Add 1 cup of the hot liquid from the crockpot to the sour cream mixture and stir until combined. Return this mixture to the crockpot and stir well.
- Cover crockpot and cook on high for 20-30 minutes until thickened and bubbly.
- I added about a tablespoon of cornstarch as a last step before eating. It was not as thick as I would have liked it.

43. Crockpot Creole Steak Strips Recipe

Serving: 6 | Prep: | Cook: 8mins | Ready in:

Ingredients

- 1 1/2 lbs. boneless round steak
- salt and pepper
- 1/2 cup chopped onion
- 1 cup sliced celery
- 1 cup V-8 juice
- 2 tsp worcestershire sauce
- 1/8 tsp garlic powder (can use fresh)
- 1 medium green bell pepper chopped
- 1 10 oz. package frozen okra (about 1 1/2 cup)
- 1 4 oz can sliced mushrooms drained
- *can add diced tomato*
- cooked rice

Direction

- Cut steak into strips 1/2 inch wide and 2 inches long.
- Sprinkle with salt and pepper.
- Put meat in crockpot with onion, celery, juice, Worcestershire sauce and garlic.
- Cover and cook on low for 6 to 8 hours.
- Turn to high.
- Add peppers, partially thawed okra and mushrooms.
- Cover and cook for 30 minutes or until okra is done.
- Serve over hot cooked rice.

44. Crockpot German Beef Recipe

Serving: 4 | Prep: | Cook: 7hours20mins | Ready in:

Ingredients

- 1 1/2 lbs beef chuck, cut in 2' cubes
- 2 tbs flour
- 1/2 tsp celery salt
- 1/2 tsp garlic powder

- 1/2 tsp ground ginger
- 1/4 tsp ground black pepper
- 1 can (16 oz) diced tomatoes, with juice
- 2 cups thinly sliced carrots
- 1 large potato, cut into chunks
- 1/4 cup sherry
- 1/4 cup dark molasses
- 1 cup water
- 1cup beer

Direction

- Place beef in crockpot. Sprinkle salt, garlic powder, ginger, pepper over top of beef. Put remaining ingredients over top of beef. Cover and cook on low for 6-8 hours.

---

45. Crockpot Mushroom Stuffed Beef Rollups Recipe

Serving: 4 | Prep: | Cook: 420mins | Ready in:

Ingredients

- $ thin beef round steaks (about 3 oz each)
- olive oil
- 4 oz mushrooms, chopped
- 1 onion, chopped
- 1 rib celery, chopped
- 1 cup seasoned stuffing mix
- 2 cups beef broth
- 1 Tbl dry red wine
- 1 bay leaf
- 3 Tbl COLD water
- 2 Tbl cornstarch
- black pepper to taste

Direction

- Using a meat mallet, pound steaks to 1/4 inch thickness.
- Coat a nonstick skillet with olive oil and heat over medium high heat. Add the mushrooms, onions, and celery, and sauté, stirring until the mushrooms and onions are lightly browned.

- In a bowl, combine the mushroom mixture, stuffing mix, and 1/2 cup of the broth. Place a spoonful of the stuffing mixture in the center of each steak, roll up, and secure with a toothpick.
- Heat the nonstick skillet again, add the roll ups, and cook until they're browned on all sides. Transfer to crockpot. Pour in the wine and the remaining 1/2 cup broth. Add the bay leaf. Cover and cook on low for 6 -8 hours, until beef is cooked through and very tender.
- Remove to a platter, reserving the broth - keep the beef warm. Discard bay leaf. Pour broth into a saucepan.
- Combine the cornstarch and cold water in a measuring cup. Pour into the broth and cook, stirring, over medium heat until thickened, about 2 minutes. Serve the roll ups with the thickened broth. If desired, sprinkle pepper over each serving.

---

46. Crockpot Pasta Laya As In Jambalaya Recipe

Serving: 1012 | Prep: | Cook: 390mins | Ready in:

Ingredients

- 1-lb smoked sausage sliced into 1/4-inch rounds
- 1/2-lb boneless pork chops, cubed
- 1-lb boneless chicken, cut into cubes, boneless thighs have more flavor
- 1 ½-cups chopped onions
- 1 bell pepper, chopped
- 1-rib celery, chopped
- 2-tsp. Minced garlic
- 1-tbsp. worcestershire sauce
- 1-tbsp. creole seasoning (I use Tony Chacherie's)
- 1 can Rotel tomatoes
- 1-can stewed tomatoes
- 1(8-oz) can tomato sauce
- 2-cups water

- 1-lb cooked spaghetti

Direction

- Brown down the sausage, drain and put into the slow cooker. Brown the chicken and pork in the grease left over from the sausage and place in slow cooker.
- (Add a little olive oil if needed.)
- Sauté onions, bell pepper, celery and garlic in same pan.
- Drain off any excess oil and add Worcestershire Sauce.
- Put in slow cooker.
- Add remaining ingredients except spaghetti.
- Cook on low for 6 1/2-hours.
- Serve over spaghetti.
- (Makes enough for 12 or more with a side salad added.)
- Susana

47. Crockpot Peking Pork Chops Recipe

Serving: 2 | Prep: | Cook: 6hours25mins | Ready in:

Ingredients

- 6 pork chops, about 1 inch thick
- Sauce:
- 1/4 cup brown sugar
- 1 teaspoon ground ginger
- 1/2 cup soy sauce
- 1/4 cup ketchup
- 1 to 2 cloves garlic, mashed
- salt and pepper to taste

Direction

- Trim excess fat from pork chops. Place pork chops in crockpot. Mix sauce ingredients together. Pour mixture over meat in crockpot.
- Cook, covered, on low for 4 to 6 hours, or until tender.
- Season with salt and pepper.

- Serve with: steamed white rice or jasmine rice and/or Chinese noodles.

48. Crockpot Round Steak With Gravy Recipe

Serving: 4 | Prep: | Cook: 9mins | Ready in:

Ingredients

- 1 Package boneless round steak
- 1 Small Can cream of mushroom soup
- 1/4 C water
- 1/2 packet of onion soup mix

Direction

- Place all ingredients into crockpot or slow cooker.
- Set on low.
- Allow to cook 8-10 hours.
- Steak will fall apart when done.
- Pairs well over cooked white/brown rice or with egg noodles.

49. Crockpot Sour Cream Pork Chops Recipe

Serving: 6 | Prep: | Cook: 15mins | Ready in:

Ingredients

- 6 pork chops
- salt and pepper, to taste
- garlic powder, to taste
- 1/2 cup flour
- 1 large onion, sliced 1/4" thick
- 8 ozs. fresh mushrooms, sliced
- 1 chicken bouillon cube
- 1 cup boiling water
- 1 can cream of mushroom soup
- 1 8 oz. carton of sour cream

Direction

- Season pork chops with salt, pepper and garlic powder, and then dredge in flour. In a skillet over medium heat, lightly brown chops in a small amount of oil.
- In the bottom of a crockpot, place the onion and mushroom slices, topped with the pork chops.
- In a medium bowl, dissolve bouillon cube; stir in cream of mushroom soup. Pour over pork chop. Cover, and cook on LOW 7-8 hours.
- Preheat oven to 200*.
- After the chops have cooked, transfer the pork chops to the oven to keep warm. Be careful, the chops are so tender that will fall apart. Add the sour cream to the contents inside the crockpot. Stir well. Turn crockpot on HIGH for 20 minutes to warm sauce. Serve the sauce over the pork chops, and noodles or rice.

50. Crockpot Swiss Steak Recipe

Serving: 4 | Prep: | Cook: 120mins | Ready in:

Ingredients

- 2 lb tenderized trimmed round steak
- 1 can diced tomatoes
- 1 can Rotel tomatoes with chiles
- 1 tsp paprika
- 2 tsp kosher salt
- 3/4 cup all purpose flour
- 1 large onion sliced
- 2 tsp minced garlic
- 1/4 cup vegetable oil
- 1 tsp oregano
- 1 tsp ground black pepper
- 1 tablespoon worcestershire sauce
- 2 cups beef broth
- preheat oven t0 325 degrees F

Direction

- Cut the meat with the grain into 1/2-inch thick slices and season on both sides with the salt and pepper.
- Place the flour into a pie pan. Dredge the pieces of meat on both sides in the flour mixture.
- Add vegetable oil to just cover the bottom of fry pan set over medium-high heat.
- Once the oil begins to shimmer, add the steaks to the pan, being careful not to overcrowd. Cook until golden brown on both sides, approximately 2 minutes per side.
- Remove the steaks to a plate and repeat until all of the steaks have been browned.
- Remove the last steaks from the pan and add the onions, garlic.
- Sauté for 1 to 2 minutes.
- Next add the tomatoes, paprika, oregano, Worcestershire sauce and beef broth and stir to combine (in the pan or place in bowl to mix together.
- Place meat in crockpot and cover with remaining ingredients.
- Cook on low for 6-8 hrs. or on high for 3-4 hours until meat falls apart. (Hint: use a crockpot liner for easy cleanup)

51. Cube Steaks And Gravy Recipe

Serving: 6 | Prep: | Cook: 8hours7mins | Ready in:

Ingredients

- 2.5 lbs cube steaks
- salt to taste
- pepper to taste
- flour
- 1 pkg. onion gravy mix
- 1 can cream of mushroom soup
- 2 cups water

Direction

- Salt and pepper cube steaks and dredge in flour. Fry until browned. Place in crockpot.

Mix gravy mix, soup and water and pour over steaks. Cover and cook on low for 6-8 hrs.

52. Dean Weens Sunday Pasta Sauce Recipe

Serving: 10 | Prep: | Cook: 180mins | Ready in:

Ingredients

- 4 lbs of ground beef/veal/pork (if you're lucky enough to have a butcher in your hometown have him grind it from cutlets, if not then buy it in the plastic packs)
- some pork chops (bone in)
- 2 lbs. of penne rigate
- 1 gigantic yellow onion
- 1 head of garlic
- 1 fresh batch of basil
- 1 batch fresh parsley
- 1 egg
- 1 long ring of hot italian sausage
- 4 slices of bread (any kind of white bread)
- milk
- pecorino/romano cheese (don't skip on this one, buy the best cheese you can get and either grate it or spend extra for the good stuff already grated)
- extra virgin olive oil
- dry white wine
- 3 big (29 oz.) cans of tomato sauce (depending on what texture you like—I like regular, already pureed sauce for this recipe)
- 5 1/2 C. water (you will fill the 3 tomato sauce cans up 1/2 way to get this water, will not need to measure and set aside during prep)
- 4 bottles of wine
- A loaf of fresh Italian bread, and get some butter too.
- *** I made some additions to it this evening when making it again after a long time. Here goes:
- I roasted the meatballs vs frying them (on 400 for 20 minutes), it made the whole operation much easier. Used an ice cream scoop to divvy up the meat mixture. I didnt use any veal, just 3 parts beef and one part pork.1 extra egg too. Added another can of the tomato sauce, reduced the water added to just about 1 cup, added a whole cup of wine, and also cooked all of the other meat in the pan with a lil white wine. I added about a teaspoon of thyme, salt to taste, lots of black pepper, 2 Bay Leaves.... I used chicken italian sausage instead of pork (sweet) , some red pepper flakes, 1 tbsp of Worcestershire sauce, 1/4 tsp nutmeg, and then just threw all of the stuff into the sauce. Didnt cook it for three hours, just about two so that i could freeze it and have it taste fresher when reheated. It was marvelous. Oh yeah and 1/2 jar of Newmans Own Spaghtti sauce and a little bit of sweet red pepper , about 1/2 cuo, chopped.

Direction

- Meatball Mixture: Dice 5 of the garlic cloves and the entire yellow onion, very fine. Chop the basil, all of it. Mix together and Set these aside.
- Put the beef/veal/pork/ into large bowl and add salt, pepper, a little bit of oregano, ½ cup of the cheese, and one raw egg.
- Take 4 slices of the white bread and put it into a cereal bowl and fill it with milk. This is what will make your meatballs excellent.
- Sautee ½ of your onion, garlic & basil mixture in 2 tbsps. of oil in a big pan, slowly. I mean really slowly. If you burn the garlic right here then all is lost. Be cautious and go slow and low, medium low heat. When the onions are translucent then it's ready, approx. 15 minutes. When the onion/garlic/basil mix is finished sautéing, then dump it on the bowl of meat. Squeeze out the milk bread and put the wrung-out milk bread into the meat bowl too. Squeeze the milk bread gently so it relinquishes half of the absorbed milk. Go easy.
- Knead the meat mixture for 5 minutes, getting it thoroughly blended. Set aside.

- The Sauce: Add another 2 tablespoons of olive oil to a large spaghetti pot and sauté the rest of your onions, garlic and basil, again, slow and low. Do not burn the garlic.
- When the onions are translucent, add the three cans of tomato sauce. For every can that you pour in the pot, go to the sink and fill up 1/2 the can with water and dump it in the pot, rinsing out the remaining sauce still in the can. 3 cans of tomato sauce, 1 ½ cans of water.
- Now sprinkle oregano on the pot of sauce, and add a tablespoon of sugar, stir it a little, and simmer the sauce on medium low heat.
- Meatballs: Brown meatballs before putting them in the sauce. Pour an inch of oil in the bottom of your pan and turn the burner to medium high. Get oil scorching hot. Shape the meatballs in your hand to whatever size you like. Add them to the scorching hot pan, try and not let them touch one another. If the oil is hot they should brown on each side quickly. We are not trying to cook them here, it's okay if they're still undercooked in the middle, they will be cooking in the sauce for three hours. When each side is browned, remove the meatballs to some paper towels and add the next batch to your pan. I usually have to do this 4 times, 4 batches of meatballs. When you're done, add your browned meatballs to the sauce.
- Pork Chops: You can throw a couple of (bone in) pork chops into Sunday sauce, they add a ton of flavor and they completely fall apart while cooking in the tomato sauce. Anyway, using the same oil you used for the meatballs, brown your pork chops, remove them from the pan and pat some of the oil off with a paper towel and then add them to the tomato sauce too.
- Sausage: After this, cook the sausage and repeat the previous, add the sausage into the sauce. It too helps the flavor of the sauce.
- Deglazing the pan: By now the bottom of your pan is filled with little bits of meatball, pork chop, sausage, onions, etc. put the empty oily pan back onto medium high heat and pour in some wine, enough to cover the bottom and

then a little more. Smoke will come billowing out and all of the pieces that were stuck to the bottom will come off. Simmer this for a couple of minutes until the alcohol cooks off, you will be able to smell this. Now pour the brownish wine gravy into your sauce and stir it in.
- The hard work is now over. You are going to let your sauce simmer on low heat for the next three hours. Stir it at regular intervals to prevent it from burning on the bottom. Clean up the mess that you've created and get ready for the final phase. Over the next three hours your sauce is going to relinquish a lot of fat and oil, like tons of it. Try to skim 90 percent of it off. It is a constant job. Some people believe in stirring it back in for flavor. You will see what I mean. Leave some and stir it back in, but not a whole lot.
- Cook your Penne pasta until it is al-dente, about 11 or 12 minutes. When it's finished, drain it in a colander and then transfer it to a big serving plate. A large plate is better than a bowl for this.
- Grab a fistful of cheese and cover the pasta with it and then toss it a little, this will help the sauce adhere to the pasta.
- Now start spooning the tomato sauce over the pasta, stirring it in, covering the pasta. Don't put too much sauce on it yet, let your guests decide how much they want, I just cover it enough to use as a starting point.
- You can put some meat around the outer ring of the serving plate, but take the whole pot of sauce and meat and put that on the table too. Let people decide how much sauce they like and let them hand pick what meatballs, sausage, and pork they want.
- Last but not least, sprinkle the dish with parsley and a little more cheese for presentation. You made it.

53. EASY CROCK CHOPS Recipe

Serving: 6 | Prep: | Cook: 360mins | Ready in:

Ingredients

- 6 boneless pork chops
- 1/4 C. brown sugar
- 1/2 tsp. cinnamon
- 1/4 tsp. ground cloves
- 1-8 oz. can tomato sauce
- 1-29 oz. can peach halves
- 1/4 C. vinegar
- salt and pepper to taste

Direction

- Lightly brown chops on both sides in skillet.
- Pour off excess fat.
- Combine brown sugar, cinnamon, cloves, tomato sauce, vinegar and 1/4 cup of syrup from peaches.
- Sprinkle chops with salt and pepper.
- Arrange chops in crock.
- Place drained peaches on top.
- Pour tomato mixture over all.
- Cover and cook on low for 6 hours.

54. EASY CROCK POT PORK CHOPS Recipe

Serving: 6 | Prep: | Cook: 360mins |Ready in:

Ingredients

- 6 pork chops of your choice
- 2 Tbs. or more flour
- 1 can chicken Rice soup

Direction

- Dredge the pork chops in the flour and brown in a skillet with oil.
- Place pork chops into Crock pot and pour the can of soup over the pork chops.
- DO NOT ADD WATER!
- Cook on High for 2-3 hours or low for about 5 hours.

- You can also pour in a box of stuffing mix and add 1/4 cup of water and have pork chops and stuffing.

55. Easy As Beef Bourguignon Recipe

Serving: 4 | Prep: | Cook: 24mins |Ready in:

Ingredients

- 2T   butter
- 2T   oil
- 2   small onions quartered
- 2   cloves garlic, crushed
- 4-6   rashers bacon, chopped
- 3/4kg chuck or round steak, cut in 2cm cubes
- 4T   flour
- 1tsp   thyme
- 1tsp   oregano
- 1T   tomato paste
- 1c   beef stock
- 1c   red wine (I use 1/2c wine and add an extra 1/2c stock)
- 250g sliced mushrooms

Direction

- Heat butter and oil in pan. Add onion, garlic and chopped bacon. Sauté until onions are tender.
- Dust meat in flour and add to pan. Cook until meat is browned.
- Transfer to a slow cooker and add remaining ingredients.
- Cover and cook on low 8-10 hours or on high 4-5 hours.
- Season to taste and serve with mashed potatoes or rice.

56. Easy Breezy Beautiful Porkchop Girl Recipe

Serving: 8 | Prep: | Cook: 120mins | Ready in:

Ingredients

- pork chops
- mushroom soup (any brand)
- pepper
- garlic powder
- onion powder
- Crushed Chillies
- butter or margarine

Direction

- Turn Crock pot on High
- Add pack of Porkchops (usually 8)
- Empty two cans of Mushroom soup on top
- Grind pepper and add all herbs/ spices
- Dab a blob of butter on top.
- Put lid on and leave for two hours- then serve!

57. Easy Cranberry Pork Chops Recipe

Serving: 0 | Prep: | Cook: 20mins | Ready in:

Ingredients

- 4 or 6 pork chops
- 1 (16 ounce) canned cranberry sauce
- 1/2 cup apple juice
- 1 tbsp apple cider vinegar
- 2 tbsp brown sugar
- 2 tbsp wholegrain mustard
- 2 tbsp cornstarch
- 1/4 cup cold water

Direction

- Combine cranberry sauce, juice, apple cider vinegar, brown sugar and mustard until

smooth; pour over chops. (Prepare to this stage when using a crock pot liner bag)
- Cover and cook on LOW for 7 to 8 hours or until meat is tender.
- Remove chops and keep warm.
- In a saucepan, combine cornstarch and cold water until smooth; and then gradually stir in cooking juices. Bring to a boil; cook and stir for 2 minutes or until thickened. Season to taste. Serve over chops.

58. Easy Crockpot Beef Stroganoff Recipe

Serving: 6 | Prep: | Cook: 8mins | Ready in:

Ingredients

- 2 lbs sirloin tips
- extra virgin olive oil
- Seasoned salt
- garlic pepper
- Unseasoned meat tenderizer
- worcestershire sauce
- Montreal steak seasoning
- 1/2 pkg dry beefy onion soup mix (or onion)
- 2 T minced onion
- 1 can sliced musrooms, drained
- 1 can mushroom soup
- 2 soup cans water (or, one soup can beef stock and one soup can water)
- 4 T sour cream
- 2 T cornstarch
- 2 T water
- Minute Rice or egg noodles, (cooked according to directions, for six servings)

Direction

- Lightly drizzle a little extra virgin olive oil over beef tips, and season well with seasonings
- Place in slow cooker

- Stir together Mushrooms, onion, soup, water/beef stock, dry soup mix and pour over meat
- Cook on low 6-8 hours
- ** If my meat is frozen, I leave it that way. It will be nice and brown and tender when you get home from work. Just cut back a little on the water **
- Remove slow cooker from base and place on stovetop, OR Transfer beef and sauce to stove top pot just before serving and bring to low boil
- Mix together the cornstarch and 2 T water
- Pour into pot and stir to thicken gravy
- Remove from heat and stir in sour cream
- Serve over rice or noodles

59. Easy Crockpot Beef Tips And Gravy Recipe

Serving: 6 | Prep: | Cook: 480mins |Ready in:

Ingredients

- 1 1/2 pounds beef stew meat, sirloin tips or chuck steak chunks
- 2 T. olive or other oil for browning
- 1 packet au jus mix, low sodium if available!
- 2 packets brown gravy mix, low sodium if available!
- Your favorite seasonings (no salt)
- 2 cups water, divided
- wide egg noodles or other choice of starch to serve

Direction

- Heat medium skillet to med-high heat, and brown tips lightly in oil.
- Transfer to crockpot.
- Mix "au jus" packet mix with 1 1/2 cups water, stir well and pour over beef tips.
- Add seasonings of your choice, such as black pepper, garlic, or herbs. Do not use salt---the packets are salty enough!

- Place lid on crock pot and cook on slow for 7 hours, or high for 5 hours.
- Mix the two brown gravy packets with another 1/2 cup COOL water, stirring well.
- Add gravy mix to crockpot, and let heat on high for about 30-40 minutes more.
- Remove lid, stir and cool down slightly before serving over noodles, mashed potatoes, or rice.
- Enjoy!

60. Easy Mexican Style Tri Tip For Burritos Or Enchiladas Recipe

Serving: 8 | Prep: | Cook: 360mins |Ready in:

Ingredients

- 1 large tri-tip roast, well-trimmed of excess fat
- 1, 28 ounce can of diced, chopped or tomato strips with basil
- 1 large package of taco seasoning (I prefer Lawry's blend)
- 2 medium white or yellow onions, chopped
- *Optional: if you want to add some heat to the recipe, add a few sliced jalapeno peppers or some chipolte peppers, chopped and seeded.

Direction

- Turn on the crockpot to High.
- On your stove, brown the tri-tip in a pan without oil until lightly browned on both sides.
- Place beef in crockpot.
- Cover the beef with the canned tomatoes then sprinkle with the taco seasoning.
- Sprinkle the chopped onions over the seasonings and cover the pot.
- Cook for at least six hours until tender.
- When the beef is tender, remove from crockpot and chop, shred or slice. (If the meat isn't tender, return cut beef back into the pot and cook for 30 minutes to an hour longer.)

- The beef is now ready to be used in your favorite recipes. Use the sauce, too as it's full of flavor!
- *** I cook 2 tri-tips at the same time. I chop up one for burritos or enchiladas and save the other one which can be used like a pot roast or frozen for another meal. This beef is great when sliced and served on rolls for sandwiches.
- You can also just slice and serve the beef as it is. Serve a few slices over some white rice and spoon some of the sauce over the top of the beef.
- Also, you can cook this in the oven using a Dutch oven or casserole dish. Bake at 350 for four hours. I'm sure that you pressure cooker folks out there could do this in your pressure cooker as well. Just don't add any liquids as the canned tomatoes give the meat just enough sauce to cook in.
- Our Favorite Burritos Recipe...
- Using large flour tortillas (the huge ones for burritos), heat up your tortilla in a large frying pan until it is warm and a few large bubbles form in the middle of the tortilla.
- Spread the tortilla with warmed refried beans on one half of the tortilla. Sprinkle with shredded Monterey Jack cheese. Place the hot shredded beef over the cheese. Sprinkle with freshly chopped tomatoes, onions and cilantro. Add a few teaspoons of sour cream and roll up and seal.
- Serve on a plate next to a small salad with a few tablespoonfuls of bottled salsa on top and some freshly-cooked corn OR a large good scoop of refried beans sprinkled with shredded cheese.
- And yes, you can make this with chicken! Try using six to eight chicken breasts. You can use the frozen breasts or tenders that come in those large plastic bags or fresh breasts. The cooking time will be about four hours with a crockpot set on high. You can cook this all day on low, too. Happy munching!

61. Forget About It Spicy Pork Tacos Recipe

Serving: 8 | Prep: | Cook: 360mins | Ready in:

Ingredients

- pork - I used a couple pounds pork sirloin boneless chops - any pork will do
- salsa of your choice - I used Herdez 5 Chile salsa (about half a jar)
- 1 cup chopped onion
- 1 Tbls lime juice
- THAT'S IT!!!

Direction

- Place chopped onion in crockpot
- Add pork
- Pour salsa and lime juice over
- Set on high for a little while till hot then switch to low for up to 8 hrs. (doesn't take that long)

62. Garlic Beef Stroganoff In The Crock Pot Recipe

Serving: 4 | Prep: | Cook: 480mins | Ready in:

Ingredients

- 2 teaspoons beef bouillon granules
- 1 cup boiling water
- 1 can condensed cream of mushroom soup undiluted
- 2 jars sliced mushrooms drained
- 1 large white onion chopped
- 3 cloves garlic minced
- 1 tablespoon worcestershire sauce
- 2 pounds round steak trimmed and cut into thin strips
- 2 tablespoons vegetable oil
- 8 ounces cream cheese cubed
- Hot cooked noodles

Direction

- In a slow cooker dissolve bouillon in water.
- Add soup, onion, mushrooms, garlic and Worcestershire.
- In a skillet brown beef in oil then transfer to slow cooker.
- Cover and cook on low for 8 hours.
- Stir in cream cheese until smooth then serve over hot cooked noodles.

63. Garlicked Sirloin Pot Roast Recipe

Serving: 8 | Prep: | Cook: 360mins | Ready in:

Ingredients

- 1 teaspoon salt
- 1 teaspoon freshly ground black pepper
- 1 teaspoon paprika
- 3 pound top sirloin roast
- 6 cloves garlic, slivered
- 6 yukon gold potatoes, peeled and quartered
- 4 carrots, cut into 2" pieces
- 2 large sweet onions, peeled and chopped
- 1/2 cup water
- 1/2 cup beef broth
- 3 beef bouillon cubes
- 1 bay leaf
- 2 large green bell peppers, cut into 2" pieces

Direction

- Rub meat with paprika, salt and pepper.
- Make slits in roast with a small knife.
- Insert garlic slivers into meat.
- Place the potatoes, carrots and onions in slow cooker.
- Place roast on top of the vegetables.
- Pour in water and beef broth; add bouillon cubes and bay leaf.
- Place lid on slow cooker and cook on High for 6 hours OR on Low for 8 hours.
- Add green peppers during last half hour of cooking.

64. Good Pork Chops Recipe

Serving: 8 | Prep: | Cook: 360mins | Ready in:

Ingredients

- 8 lean pork chops
- 1/2 cup flour
- 1 Tablespoon salt
- 1-1/2 teaspoons dry mustard
- 1/2 teaspoon garlic powder
- 1 can sliced mushrooms, drained
- 2 Tablespoons oil
- 1 can chicken with rice soup

Direction

- Dredge pork chops in mixture of flour, salt, dry mustard, and garlic.
- Brown in skillet with oil.
- Put chops in crockpot.
- Put soup and mushrooms in crockpot.
- Cover and cook on low 6 hours. Or high for 3 hours

65. Hawaiian Barbecued Pork Chops Slow Cooked Recipe

Serving: 0 | Prep: | Cook: 12hours | Ready in:

Ingredients

- Pre-Cooking
- 1 Bottle Lawry's teriyaki marinade (I use the one with pineapple)
- 1/4 teaspoon ground clove
- 1 teaspoon honey
- (With 8 pork steaks listed below)
- Main Ingredients
- 1 cup soy sauce(I use Aloha)
- 1/2 cup dry sherry(Optional)

- 1 cup brown sugar
- 2 cloves garlic, crushed(or 1 Tablespoon garlic powder)
- 1/4 teaspoon pepper
- 1 cup barbecue sauce (I use Tony Romas Carolina honeys)
- 1 8-ounce can pineapple chunks (do not drain)
- 1 Tablespoon grape jelly
- 8 Large pork steaks (or 16 Standard Sized pork chops)

Direction

- Prep ahead - mix marinade with ground clove and honey. Place Pork Steaks into marinade. Let stand in refrigerator for MINIMUM two hours. (or you could let them stand overnight which is what I often do).
- Combine remaining ingredients except Pork Steaks in Crock Pot and stir well. Add Pork Steaks. Stir to coat Pork Steaks.
- Cook on low, covered, for 8 to 10 hours. Serve on a bed of rice with sauce poured over.

66. Hawaiian Chop Steak Recipe

Serving: 8 | Prep: | Cook: 480mins | Ready in:

Ingredients

- 1/4 Cup olive oil
- 3 lbs round steak thinly cut 1/8" strips 3" long (no bone)
- 4 lg quartered and separated sweet white onions (Maui if you can get them)
- 6-8 lg green bell peppers (cut into strips)
- 1 Cup Janapanse style soy sauce
- 1 Cup water
- 1/2 Cup white sugar
- 1 Tbl ginger
- 1 Minced garlic clove
- 1/8 Cup sesame oil
- 2 Cups uncooked CalRose rice in 2 1/4 cups of water
- pineapple

- pickled ginger

Direction

- Heat olive oil into fry pan.
- Place beef in pan; turn beef so that each side is seared.
- Remove meat from fry pan and place into slow cooker.
- Place onions and bell peppers on top of beef.
- Mix soy sauce, water, white sugar, garlic clove and sesame oil together.
- Pour entire contents into slow cooker.
- Cook on Low 480 minutes (8 hours).
- Cook on High 180 minutes (3 hours).
- Cook rice using rice cooker or on stovetop. (Stovetop: bring to boil, cover and lower heat to slow simmer, 15 minutes; turn off heat, being careful to not remove the lid for 20 minutes).
- Place a bed of rice on each plate, put chop steak, vegetables and sauce over the rice. Place pineapple and pickled ginger on each plate.

67. Hazels Swiss Steak Recipe

Serving: 6 | Prep: | Cook: 240mins | Ready in:

Ingredients

- 2 -3 lbs round steak
- 1 1/3 c flour
- 1 tsp salt
- 1 dash pepper
- 3 Tbs oil
- 2 cups water
- 1 can cream of chicken soup
- 3 small cans tomato juice or V8
- 1 can stewed tomatoes
- 1 can cream of celery soup

Direction

- Cut meat into serving sizes.

- Dredge in flour, salt and pepper.
- Brown steaks in oil on both sides.
- Combine water, cream of chicken, cream of celery, tomatoes, and juice.
- Transfer meat to crockpot and cover with liquid mixture.
- Cook on low for 2 to 4 hours.

68. Italian Combo Subs Recipe

Serving: 6 | Prep: | Cook: 240mins | Ready in:

Ingredients

- 1 lb. boneless beef round steak, cut into thin strips
- 1 lb. italian sausage, cut into pieces
- 1 Tbs. vegetable oil
- 4 oz. mushrooms, sliced, drained
- 1 green bell pepper, cut into strips
- 26 oz. pasta sauce
- 1 sliced onion
- 2 loaves French bread, cut into 6 inch pieces, split

Direction

- 1. Heat oil in skillet. Brown beef in 2 batches. Place in crock pot.
- 2. In same skillet, brown sausage and drain. Add to crock pot.
- 3. Place peppers, onion, and mushrooms over meat. Season with salt and pepper. Top with pasta sauce. Cover; cook on low 4-6 hours. Serve in bread.

69. Korean Pork Chops Recipe

Serving: 6 | Prep: | Cook: | Ready in:

Ingredients

- 6 pork chops

- 1 tbsp Korean chile bean paste
- 3 garlic cloves, pressed
- 1/2 cup soy sauce
- 1/2 cup chicken broth
- salt and pepper, to taste

Direction

- In a slow cooker, combine together the bean paste, garlic, soy sauce, and chicken broth. Season the chops with salt and pepper, then place them in the slow cooker. Turn to coat completely with sauce, cover and cook for 5 hours on Low setting.

70. Kraut Alsatian Recipe

Serving: 8 | Prep: | Cook: 114mins | Ready in:

Ingredients

- 3 bags refrigerated sauerkraut [1 lb. each
- 1 1/2 lbs. red potatoes small [scrubbed and halved
- 6 medium sized carrots peeled and sliced 1/2 inch slices
- 1 tsp. cracked black pepper
- 2 smoked pork chops 3/4 lb. total [2 regular pork chops}
- 1 cup dry white wine
- 1 lb. smoked sausages such as knockwurst or Keilbasa
- salt to taste

Direction

- Drain Kraut thoroughly then combined with potatoes carrots and pepper in a large flame proof casserole or heavy deep pot
- Arrange both types of pork chops over sauerkraut Add wine cover tightly bring to a simmer cook 1 hour till taters are tender
- Add sausage cook 15 minutes until sausage is heated through Add Salt to taste

71. Lemon Pork Chops Recipe

Serving: 4 | Prep: | Cook: 360mins |Ready in:

Ingredients

- 4 bone-in pork chops(3/4" thick
- 1/2 tsp salt
- 1/4 tsp pepper
- 1 medium onion,cut in 1/4" slices
- 1 medium lemon,cut in 1/4" slices
- 1/4 c packed brown sugar
- 1/4 c ketchup

Direction

- Place pork chops in 3 qt. slow cooker. Sprinkle with salt and pepper. Top with onion and lemon. Sprinkle with brown sugar; drizzle with ketchup. Cover and cook on low for 6 hours or till juices run clear.

72. London Broil Strog A Noff Recipe

Serving: 4 | Prep: | Cook: 480mins |Ready in:

Ingredients

- London Broil
- Cream of Something soup (I used celery)
- milk
- onion soup mix packet
- canned mushrooms
- Onion
- garlic
- ground black pepper
- elbow macaroni (I would have preferred egg noodles)

Direction

- Chop garlic & onion & place in slow cooker. (I turn mine on high before I start chopping so it has a chance to warm up)
- Place London Broil on top of onion & garlic
- Mix together the milk (approximately 1 cup) canned soup & onion soup mix.
- Add pepper to taste.
- Cook on low all day while you are work or cleaning the house. (I started mine out on high until the cooker comes up to temperature.)
- Cook noodle on the stove, drain & add to the slow cooker. The meat will have fallen apart by now. Mix.
- I added a few tablespoons of grated pecorino for added flavor.

73. Mexicali Round Steak Recipe

Serving: 6 | Prep: | Cook: 480mins |Ready in:

Ingredients

- 1 1/2 pounds beef boneless round steak
- 1 cup frozen whole kernel corn
- 1 cup chopped fresh cilantro
- 1/2 cup beef broth
- 3 medium stalks celery, thinly sliced, about 1 1/2 cups
- 1 large onion, sliced
- 1 jar salsa (20 ounce)
- 1 can black beans (15 ounce) rinse & drained, rinse & drain again.
- 1 cup shredded monterey jack cheese with jalapeno peppers (4 ounces)

Direction

- Trim excess fat from beef. Cut into 6 serving pieces. Place beef in 3 1/2 to 6 quart slow cooker.
- Mix remaining ingredients, except cheese. Pour over beef.
- Cover and cook on low 8 - 9 hours until beef is tender.

- Sprinkle cheese over beef mixture right before serving.

74. Mountain Chili Recipe

Serving: 8 | Prep: | Cook: 2mins | Ready in:

Ingredients

- 1 pound boneless beef sirloin steak, cut into 3/4-inch cubes
- 4 italian sausage links, casings removed and cut into 3/4 inch slices
- 2 tablespoons olive oil, divided
- 1 onion, chopped
- 3 garlic cloves, minced
- 2 green onions, thinly sliced
- 2 teaspoons beef bouillion granules
- 1 cup boiling water
- 1/4 cup red wine
- 1-6 ounce can tomato paste
- 3 tablespoons chili powder
- 2 tablespoons brown sugar
- 2 tablespoons worcestershire sauce
- 2 teaspoons ground cumin
- 1-2 teaspoons crushed red pepper flakes
- salt to taste, not a lot though
- pepper to taste
- 3 cans, 14.5 ounces each, stewed tomatoes, cut up
- 2 15 ounce cans pinto beans, rinsed and drained
- 1 pound shredded sharp cheddar cheese
- sour cream
- rice or potatoes to pour it over

Direction

- In a large skillet, brown the beef and sausage in 1 tablespoon of oil.
- Drain.
- Transfer meat to a 5-quart slow cooker.
- In the same skillet you cooked the beef, sauté the onion, garlic and green onions in remaining oil until tender.

- Transfer to the slow cooker.
- In a small bowl, dissolve bouillon in water.
- Stir in wine, tomato paste, chili powder, brown sugar, Worcestershire sauce and seasonings until blended.
- Add to slow cooker.
- Stir tomatoes and beans into slow cooker.
- Cover and cook on high for 6-8 hours.
- Serve over potatoes or rice and garnish with cheese and sour cream.

75. Mustard Pork Recipe

Serving: 4 | Prep: | Cook: 8hours25mins | Ready in:

Ingredients

- 6 pork chops, browned
- 10 3/4 ounces cream of mushroom soup, canned
- 1/4 cup chicken broth
- 1/4 cup Dijon mustard
- 1 teaspoon garlic, minced
- 1/4 teaspoon pepper
- 6 potatoes, sliced
- 1 onion, sliced

Direction

- Combine ingredients in slow cooker.
- Cover; cook on Low 8-10 hours or High 4-5 hours.

76. Nonnies Slow Cook Swiss Steak Recipe

Serving: 6 | Prep: | Cook: 480mins | Ready in:

Ingredients

- 1/4 cup or more of flour
- salt

- pepper
- 1 1/2 lb bottom round steak, about 3/4 inch thick, cut into 6 pieces
- 2 Tbl EVOO
- 1 Tbl butter
- 1 Large onion, sliced
- 2-3 stalks of celery, cut up in 2" pieces
- 1 (14.5 oz.) can of stewed tomatoes, undrained
- sliced mushrooms 1 jar (optional, add during last 30 mintues)

Direction

- Mix flour, salt and pepper together in a plate.
- Heat oil/butter mixture in a 10" skillet over medium heat.
- Dredge steak in flour and cook in pan until nicely browned, turning once (about 15 minutes).
- Place beef in a 3 1/2 to 4 qt. slow cooker.
- Distribute onion and celery over beef.
- Pour entire can of tomatoes over beef and vegetables.
- Cover and cook for 7 to 8 hours or until steak is tender.
- Carefully remove steak (keep warm) and thicken gravy if desired, with a mixture of cornstarch and cold water in equal parts.

77. Not My Mamas Swiss Steak Recipe

Serving: 6 | Prep: | Cook: 22mins | Ready in:

Ingredients

- 1 and half lbs round steak
- 2 Tbls flour
- 1/4 ts thyme
- 1/8 ts garlic powder
- salt and pepper to taste
- 1/2 medium onion chopped
- 1 green pepper diced
- 1 stalk celery

- 1 carrot chopped (optional)
- 1 clove garlic chopped or 1 ts minced garlic (more if you love garlic)
- 1 (14.5oz can) stewed tomatoes
- 1/4 cup red wine (or 1/4 can beef broth)
- 1 or more Tbls worchestershire sauce

Direction

- Cut ground steak into serving sized pieces.
- Mix flour, thyme, garlic powder, salt and pepper together.
- Dredge the meat pieces through the flour mixture and place in slow cooker.
- Chop the onion, green pepper, celery and carrot if using.
- Place the onion, green pepper, celery and carrot if using on top of the meat.
- Sprinkle minced garlic over the vegetables.
- Cover this all with the can of stewed tomatoes.
- Pour the Worcestershire sauce and wine or beef broth over all.
- Cook on low for 8 to 10 hours or high for 3 to 5 hours.
- Serve with mashed potatoes or pasta or whatever your heart desires.
- Enjoy!

78. Oriental Pepper Steak Recipe

Serving: 4 | Prep: | Cook: 480mins | Ready in:

Ingredients

- 1 pound round steak
- 1 large onion, diced
- 1 green pepper, diced
- salt and pepper
- 2/3 cup soy sauce
- 2/3 cup water
- 4 cups cooked rice

Direction

- Cut round steak into small pieces; dice onion and green pepper. Place meat, onion, green pepper, and a dash of salt and pepper into crockpot. Add soy sauce and water. Cook on low setting for 8 to 10 hours.
- Sever over cooked rice.

79. Party Beef For Roast Beef N Cheese Sandwiches Recipe

Serving: 25 | Prep: | Cook: 8mins | Ready in:

Ingredients

- 5 Lb Boneless Rump roast or sirloin tip roast
- 2 -15 oz Cans chicken broth
- 1 - 15oz Can beef Consume
- 1 beef Boullion Cube
- 1 Tablespoon Brown gravy Sauce (LaChoy)
- Optional:
- rolls (your favorite)
- cheese (we use assorted variety, marble, cheddar, mozzarella, pepperjack..etc.)

Direction

- Throw it all in the crockpot on low for 8-10 hours.
- Then slice thin and serve on rolls with cheese!

80. Paulettes Slow Cooked Pork Chops Italiano Recipe

Serving: 8 | Prep: | Cook: 8mins | Ready in:

Ingredients

- 8 lean large pork chops
- Marinade:
- 2 Tablespoons extra-virgin olive oil
- 1 pack of onion soup mix

- 2 14-½ oz cans of S &W's basil & oregano & garlic diced tomatoes, un-drained
- 1 tablespoon balsamic vinegar

Direction

- Mix all marinade ingredients in a very large bowl and stir until the soup mix is blended. Then pour over the chops which have been layered on top of each other in the slow cooker.
- Set to 300 degrees or low for 6-8 hours or until the chops are done.
- Serve up with mashed potatoes of your choice or rice or risotto and applesauce.
- ********************************
- For a more rustic dish add 1 15-oz. can of Great Northern white beans that have been rinsed and drained to the marinade. Then add to the chops.

81. Pork Burritos Recipe

Serving: 14 | Prep: | Cook: 480mins | Ready in:

Ingredients

- 1 boneless pork sirloin roast (3lbs)
- 1/4 c reduced-sodium chicken broth
- 1 envelope reduced-sodium taco seasoning
- 1 Ths dried parsley flakes
- 2 garlic cloves,minced
- 1/2 tsp pepper
- 1/4 tsp salt
- 1 can (16 oz) refried beans
- 1 can (4oz) chopped green chilies
- 14 flour tortillas (8") warmed
- optioal toppings:shredded lettuce,chopped tomatoes,guacamole,reduced-fat sour cream ,reduced-fat cheddar cheese,shredded.

Direction

- Cut roast in half, place in 4 to 5 qt. slow cooker. In a small bowl, combine broth, taco

seasoning, parsley, garlic, pepper and salt. Pour over roast and cook on low for 8 to 10 hours or till meat is very tender.
- Remove pork from slow cooker, cool slightly. Shred with 2 forks; set aside. Skim fat from the liquid; stir in beans and chilies. Return pork to the slow cooker; heat through.
- Spoon 1/22 cup pork mixture down the center of each tortilla; add toppings of your choice. Fold sides and ends over filling and roll up.

82. Pork Chops Crazy Crockpot Standing Up Recipe

Serving: 4 | Prep: | Cook: 480mins | Ready in:

Ingredients

- 4 Loin pork chops -- lean
- 2 medium onions -- sliced
- 1 teaspoon butter
- salt & pepper -- to taste
- spices of your choice

Direction

- Stand chops in crock pot, thin side down. Sprinkle with salt, pepper and spices of your choice. Cover with the onion slices, which have been separated into rings. Place butter on top, and cook on LOW heat for 6 to 8 hours, or until chops are tender and onions are done. The result is moist, tender chops with a deep brown color as if broiled in the oven.

83. Pork Chops Golden Glow Recipe

Serving: 4 | Prep: | Cook: 6hours15mins | Ready in:

Ingredients

- 5 pork chops

- 1/4 cup brown sugar
- 1/2 teaspoon cinnamon
- 1/4 teaspoon cloves
- 1 8 ounce can tomato sauce
- 1 29 ounce can cling peach halves
- 1/4 cup vinegar
- salt and pepper

Direction

- Lightly brown pork chops on both sides in large skillet. Pour off excess fat. Combine brown sugar, cinnamon, cloves, tomato sauce, 1/4 cup syrup from peaches and vinegar. Sprinkle chops with salt and pepper. Arrange chops in slow cooking pot. Place drained peach halves on top. Pour tomato mixture over all. Cover and cook on low for 4 to 6 hours.

84. Pork Chops N Apples Recipe

Serving: 6 | Prep: | Cook: 360mins | Ready in:

Ingredients

- 8 pork chops
- 5 large apples(Of your choice)
- 2 Tbsp of brown sugar
- 2 1/2tsp of mustard powder
- 4 cloves
- 1/2 tsp of Chinese five spice
- 1 cup of chicken stock
- 1 1/2 jars of chunky apple sauce
- salt and pepper
- butter to sauté

Direction

- Sauté onion and apples then place in slow cooker.
- Brown pork chops, then add to pot.
- Pour in apple sauce, juice and spices over the chops.
- Cook on high for 5-6 hours.

- When tender remove chops and keep warm, pour remaining juices from the slow cooker through a strainer.
- Keep the remaining chunks of onion and apple and 1/2 the juice.
- Pour into hot pan and reduce to desired consistency.
- Serve with mash and vegies and the apple sauce.
- ENJOY!!!!

85. Pork Chops With Cranberry Thyme Sauce Recipe

Serving: 4 | Prep: | Cook: 4hours25mins | Ready in:

Ingredients

- 1/2 cup butter, melted
- 4 boneless pork chops, 6 ounces each
- 1 cup white wine
- 1 cup cranberry sauce
- 1 small onion, chopped
- 1/4 cup fresh thyme, chopped
- salt and pepper, to taste

Direction

- Lightly brown the pork chops in a skillet.
- In a small bowl, combine the butter, cranberry sauce and white wine.
- Arrange the pork chops in the bottom of the stoneware. Sprinkle the salt and pepper, onions and thyme over the pork chops.
- Pour the sauce into the stoneware and cook on Low for 6 to 8 hours or on High for 4 to 6 hours.

86. Pork Chops With Potatoes And Kraut Recipe

Serving: 0 | Prep: | Cook: 52mins | Ready in:

Ingredients

- 6-8 pork chops
- 4 lg potatoes, peeled and sliced
- 1 lg onion, chopped
- 1 can sauerkraut, or more

Direction

- Brown pork chops in a large skillet. Add onions, potatoes, and kraut with juice. Add some additional water, about 1/2 -3/4 cup. Simmer over medium heat, covered with potatoes until potatoes are done.
- *For a crockpot, brown pork chops. Place them in the bottom of the crockpot. Top with onions, potatoes, kraut and juice. Add some additional water. Cook all day on low.

87. Pork Chops In Orange Juice Recipe

Serving: 2 | Prep: | Cook: 120mins | Ready in:

Ingredients

- 4 pork chops, center cut
- flour
- salt and pepper
- 2-3 tbsp, cooking oil
- 2 cups, orange juice

Direction

- Defrost your pork chops. Add salt and pepper to taste.
- Coat the pork chops in flour. Shake off any excess flour.
- Fry the pork chops in a frying pan with the oil till golden brown. At this point, you're just creating a crust on the exterior of the pork chops.
- Turn down the heat to medium and add 1 1/2 cups of the orange juice. Let simmer.

- Turn down the heat to low and cook for 2 hours. After 1 1/2 hours, add the rest of the orange juice if needed.

88. Pork Chops With Apples Sweet Potatoes And Sauerkraut Recipe

Serving: 4 | Prep: | Cook: 300mins | Ready in:

Ingredients

- 4 (1 inch thick) boneless pork chops
- 2 medium sweet potatoes, peeled and sliced 1/2 inch thick
- 1 medium onion, sliced
- 2 apples - peeled, cored and sliced
- 1 tablespoon brown sugar
- 1/2 teaspoon ground nutmeg
- 1/4 teaspoon salt
- freshly ground black pepper to taste
- 1 (16 ounce) can sauerkraut, drained

Direction

- Heat a skillet over medium-high heat and coat with cooking spray.
- Quickly brown the pork chops on each side.
- Set aside.
- Arrange sweet potato slices in the bottom of a 3 to 4 quart slow cooker.
- Cover with the onion slices, then the apple slices.
- Sprinkle brown sugar, nutmeg and salt over the apples, and grind a little pepper.
- Place the pork chops on top of the pile, and cover with sauerkraut.
- Cover, and cook on Low for about 5 hours.
- Serve pork and vegetables with juice from the slow cooker spooned over them.

89. Pork Marrakesh Recipe

Serving: 4 | Prep: | Cook: 6mins | Ready in:

Ingredients

- 2 tsp olive oil
- 4 (1/4 lb) boneless pork chops, trimmed
- 3/4 tsp salt
- 1/4 tsp pepper
- 3 small red onions, thinly sliced
- 12 dried apricots, sliced
- 3/4 C unsweetened apple juice
- 2 tsp minced, peeled fresh ginger
- 1/2 tsp thyme
- 1 (inch) cinnamon stick
- 1/4 C chopped fresh cilantro or parsley

Direction

- Heat 1 tsp. oil in a large skillet over medium high heat
- Sprinkle the chops with 1/4 tsp. salt and pepper
- Add the chops to the skillet and cook until browned, about 2 minutes on each side and transfer to a plate
- Reduce the heat to medium and add the onions, the remaining 1 tsp. oil and the remaining 1/2 tsp. salt to the skillet
- Cook, stirring, until the onions are golden, about 10 minutes
- Place half the apricots and half the onion in the bottom of a slow cooker
- Top with the chops and remaining apricots and onions
- Add the apple juice, ginger, thyme and cinnamon stick
- Cover and cook until the pork in tender, 3-4 hours on high or 6-8 hours on low
- Remove the cinnamon stick and serve sprinkled with cilantro or parsley

90. Pork Stroganoff Crock Pot Cookin Recipe

Serving: 6 | Prep: | Cook: 480mins | Ready in:

Ingredients

- 3-4 boneless pork tenderloin chops, trimmed of any visible fat
- 1 can Campbell's Cream of chicken or mushroom soup
- 1 teaspoon thyme leaves
- 1/2 teaspoon dried basil
- 1 cup sharp cheddar cheese, grated
- 1/2 cup milk
- salt and pepper to taste
- egg noodles, cooked

Direction

- Spray crockpot with non-stick spray
- Place the pork chops in the bottom of the crockpot
- Top chops with the condensed soup, thyme, and basil
- Cook on low 6 to 8 hours
- Remove pork chops and shred, set aside
- In crockpot add cheese. Stir until melted.
- Add in milk and stir until smooth and gravy consistency.
- Stir back in the shredded pork.
- While shredded pork and sauce is warming in crockpot cook a bag of egg noodles according to directions on the bag.
- When noodles are done, drain and stir in to the pork mixture.
- Add salt and pepper to taste.

91. Pork Tenderloin With Mustard Sauce

Serving: 8 | Prep: | Cook: 480mins | Ready in:

Ingredients

- ⅓ cup red wine
- ⅓ cup soy sauce
- 2 tablespoons light brown sugar
- 2 pounds pork tenderloin
- ⅓ cup mayonnaise
- ⅓ cup sour cream
- 1 ½ tablespoons mustard powder
- 1 tablespoon minced fresh chives

Direction

- Combine wine, soy sauce, and brown sugar in a large resealable plastic bag. Place tenderloin in bag, and refrigerate overnight, or at least 8 hours.
- In a small bowl, combine mayonnaise, sour cream, mustard powder; mix well. Mix in minced chives if you wish. Chill until ready to serve.
- Preheat oven to 325 degrees F (165 degrees C). Place meat and marinade in a shallow baking dish, and roast for 1 hour, basting occasionally. Temperature of meat should register 145 degrees F (63 degrees C). Let rest for a few minutes, then cut into 1/2 inch thick slices. Serve with mustard sauce.
- Notes: The sauce is best if made several hours, or even a day in advance, to let the flavors blend well. You may need to adjust the amount of dry mustard to suit your taste - best to start with less, and add more if needed.
- Nutrition Facts
- Per Serving:
- 258.5 calories; protein 25g 50% DV; carbohydrates 5.5g 2% DV; fat 13.9g 21% DV; cholesterol 81.4mg 27% DV; sodium 718.8mg 29% DV.

92. Pork In Chile Sauce Recipe

Serving: 2 | Prep: | Cook: 360mins | Ready in:

Ingredients

- 1 large tomato, cored and chopped

- 1c no-salt-added tomato puree
- 1 small poblano chile, cored, seeded and chopped (see note)
- 1 large shallot or 1/2 small onion, chopped
- 1 clove garlic, minced
- 1/8t chipotle chili powder or regular chili powder
- 1/4t dried oregano, crushed
- 1/8t black pepper
- 6oz boneless pork chop, cut into 1" chunks
- 1/4t salt (optional)
- 2 warm corn or whole-wheat tortillas (optional)

Direction

- Place all but tortillas in slow cooker; mix well. Cook on low 5-6 hours. Serve with tortillas if desired.
- Note: For a moderately hot flavor, use 1/4c chopped poblano.
- Works best in 1.5qt slow cooker
- Serves 2: calories 217, fat 7g (28%), protein 22g, carbs 20g, chol 54mg, fiber 3g, sodium 89mg

93. Pork With Grapefruit Salsa Recipe

Serving: 6 | Prep: | Cook: 480mins |Ready in:

Ingredients

- 6 boneless loin pork chops
- 2 tbsp flour
- salt & pepper to taste
- 2 tbsp olive oil
- 2 onions, sliced
- 1/2 cup grapefruit juice
- 3 pink grapefruit, chopped
- 1/2 cup chopped green onions
- 1 red bell pepper, chopped
- 2 jalapeno peppers, minced
- 1 tbsp sugar
- 1/8 tsp cayenne pepper

- 1/4 cup chopped cilantro

Direction

- DIR
- Sprinkle pork chops with flour, salt and pepper.
- Heat olive oil in large skillet.
- Brown chops on both sides, about 5 minutes total.
- Layer with onions in slow cooker.
- Pour grapefruit juice over all.
- Cover & cook on LOW for 7 to 8 hours, or until meat is tender and registers 155*F on meat thermometer.
- Meanwhile, make the salsa:
- In medium sized bowl, combine all remaining ingredients and mix well.
- Cover & chill until pork chops are ready.

94. Ranch Pork Chops Recipe

Serving: 0 | Prep: | Cook: 6hours5mins |Ready in:

Ingredients

- pork chops
- Ranch seasoning Dry Mix Packet
- 1 can Cream of chicken plus 1 can water as needed {or 2 cans cream of chicken}

Direction

- Combine all three ingredients in the crock-pot and mix well.

95. Rich Texas Chili Recipe

Serving: 6 | Prep: | Cook: 240mins |Ready in:

Ingredients

- 3 lbs good quality chuck steak, NY strip with fat trimmed off
- 1 large yellow onion
- 1/8 cup corn oil
- 3 cloves garlic
- 3 tablespoon corn flour
- 2 tablespoons chili powder
- 2 tablespoon paprika
- 1 teaspoon cumin
- 1/2 teaspoon oregano
- 1 can tomato paste
- 1 can large can chopped tomatoes
- 2 cups low salt beef stock
- 2 dashes Tabasco sauce
- 2 chipotle peppers

Direction

- Cut steak into 1/4" cubes; dredge in corn flour.
- In heavy skillet, heat 1/2 corn oil till hot, work in 2 batches, brown beef; after second batch, brown onions; add garlic but do not brown.
- Place meat, onions, garlic in slow cooker.
- Fry tomato paste in same skillet until caramelized; add to slow cooker along with remaining ingredients. Cook on low for 6 hours or until thick and meat is tender. Adjust seasoning. Taste even better the second day. Enjoy!

96. Royal Roundsteak Recipe

Serving: 6 | Prep: | Cook: 360mins | Ready in:

Ingredients

- 1-2 lbs. round steak or beef stew meat
- 1-2 T oil
- 1 Envelope (10oz) onion soup mix
- 2 Cans Cream of mushroom
- Hot noodles or rice

Direction

- Heat oil in a skillet over medium heat, add meat and brown till done.
- In a bowl, combine soup mix and cream soup.
- Pour soup mixture into crockpot, add browned meat.
- Cook in crockpot on LOW 6-7 hours.
- Serve over hot noodles or rice.

97. Salsa Swiss Steak Recipe

Serving: 6 | Prep: | Cook: 22mins | Ready in:

Ingredients

- boneless beef top round steak - 2-lbs
- large green and/or red peppers, seeded and cut into strips - 2
- medium onion, sliced - 1
- cream of mushroom soup - 1 can
- bottled salsa of choice - 1 cup
- all purpose flour - 2-tbspn
- dry mustard - 1 tspn

Direction

- Cut steak into 6-12 pieces and put into crockpot.
- Add sweet peppers and onion.
- In a medium bowl, stir together soup, salsa, flour, and mustard.
- Pour over steak and vegetables in slow cooker.
- Cover and cook on low for 9 hours.
- NOTE: I made some rice and serve cornbread and turnip greens for a side. So-o-o good.
- -Susana

98. Savory Pepper Steak Recipe

Serving: 4 | Prep: | Cook: 8hours | Ready in:

Ingredients

- 1 1/2 lbs round steak cut into strips

- 1/4 cup flour
- 1/2 tsp salt
- 1/2 tsp pepper
- 1 small onion
- 4-5 garlic cloves
- 1 green pepper
- 1 red pepper
- 16 oz can Italian style tomatoes
- 1 tbsp. beef bouillon
- 2 tbsp. worcestershire sauce
- 1 tbsp. steak seasoning
- 1 tbsp. steak sauck

Direction

- Toss steak in salt, pepper, & flour and add to gallon-sized freezer bags. Mix together rest of ingredient and add to bag.
- Thaw overnight
- Cook on low for 8 hours

99. Savoury Crock Pot Pepper Steak Recipe

Serving: 6 | Prep: | Cook: 3mins | Ready in:

Ingredients

- 2lbs round steak cut in 1"strips
- 1 can tomatoes undrained
- onion
- garlic
- flour
- salt and pepper
- 2tsp worchistire sauce
- ttbsp soy
- 1tbsp beef flavour base
- red and green peppers
- 2 cups hot rice

Direction

- 2lbs beef round steak 1/2 inch thick
- 1/4 cup flour
- 1/2 tsp salt

- 1/8tsp pepper
- 1 medium onion
- 1 small clove garlic both minced/chopped
- 2 large bell red/green peppers
- Seeded and cut to strips
- 1 can whole tomatoes undrained
- 1 tbsp. beef flavor base
- 1tbsp soy sauce
- 2tsp Worchester sauce
- Serve on hot cooked rice
- Cut steak into strips. Combine flour salt and pepper and toss steak to coat well and put in crock pot
- Put onion, garlic and half of the peppers on and stir
- Combine tomatoes with beef base, soy and worcheshire and pour on
- Cook on low for 8-10 hours
- One hour before serving turn on high and stir in rest of peppers
- If want a thick gravy, make a smooth paste of 3 tbsp flour and 3 tbsp water, stir in crock, cook and cover till thick

100. Sirloin Tips And Rice Recipe

Serving: 8 | Prep: | Cook: 360mins | Ready in:

Ingredients

- 1 or 2 lbs sirloin steak-cut bite size
- 1 pkg onion soup mix
- 1 can Golden mushroom soup
- 4 oz mushrooms with juice
- 1/2 c red bell pepper-chopped   (I leave this out)
- 4 green onions-chopped
- 2 cloves of garlic or 1 t garlic powder
- salt & pepper
- 3 c hot cooked rice-made last 20 minutes of cook time

Direction

- Season steak lightly and put in crockpot. Mix soup, dry soup, and garlic in a bowl. Pour on steak. Top with the remaining ingredients and stir all to blend. Cover and cook low for 6-8 hours or high for 4-5 hours. Cook rice the last 20 minutes of cook time and serve tips and gravy over rice. I have made this with egg noodles and/or mashed potatoes.

101. Sirloin Tips With Caramelized Onion Brandy Sauce Recipe

Serving: 4 | Prep: | Cook: 360mins | Ready in:

Ingredients

- 3 tbsp all purpose flour
- 1/2 tsp salt
- 1/2 tsp black pepper
- 1 1/2 pounds beef sirloin tips, cut into 2 inch pieces
- 1/2 cup beef broth
- 3 tbsp brandy
- 1 tsp worcestershire sauce
- 1 clove garlic, minced
- 2 tbsp butter, melted (I just use olive oil)
- 1 tbsp packed brown sugar
- 1/4 tsp ground red pepper
- 1 medium sweet onion, sliced thinly and separated into rings
- 1/4 cup heavy cream (optional)
- 1/2 cup crumbled gorgonzola cheese(optional)
- 2 tsp parsley, chopped finely(optional)

Direction

- Combine flour, salt and peppercorns. Add beef and coat with flour mixture. Do not skip this step. It's what will make the sauce. Transfer to crock pot.
- Combine broth, brandy, Worcestershire sauce and garlic in small bowl. Pour over beef.

- Combine butter (or olive oil), brown sugar and red pepper in small bowl. Add onion and transfer to crock pot. Cover and cook on low 6-8 hours or high 3-4 hours.
- You can stop here and serve. But if not, you would turn the crock pot to high and stir in heavy cream, cover, and cook for 15 minutes longer. Garnish with cheese and parsley.
- Serve with wild rice, white rice or mashed potatoes.
- I hope you enjoy it! We do.

102. Slow Cooked Apple Pear And Apricot Pork Chops Recipe

Serving: 6 | Prep: | Cook: 22mins | Ready in:

Ingredients

- 6 Smithfield pork chops
- 1 cup fresh Anjou pear -- roughly chopped
- 1 cup red apple -- roughly chopped
- 1 cup dried apricots -- chopped
- 1 medium onion -- chopped
- 3 ribs celery -- roughly sliced
- 1 tablespoon fresh thyme leaves
- 3/4 cups apple juice
- 1/2 cup dark brown sugar
- 1/4 cup white wine
- salt and pepper to taste
- 2 tablespoons cornstarch mixed with 2 tablespoons water
- Apple and pear slices for garnish

Direction

- In a slow cooker, or Dutch oven combine all ingredients, except cornstarch and water. Cover and cook on LOW for 7 to 9 hours, or 3 1/2 to 4 1/2 hours on HIGH. 30 minutes before serving, skim off any excess fat.
- Stir in cornstarch mixture and return broth to slow cooker. Continue cooking on low until sauce is smooth and thickened.
- Garnish with apple and pear slices.

- Serving Suggestions:
- Serve alongside a fresh green salad.

103.   Slow Cooked Flank Steak Recipe

Serving: 5 | Prep: | Cook: 420mins | Ready in:

Ingredients

- 1 flank steak (about 1-1/2 pounds), cut in half
- 1 tbsp. olive oil
- 1 large onion, sliced
- 1/3 cup water
- 1 can (4 ounces) chopped creen chilies
- 2 tbsp vinegar
- 1-1/4 tsp garlic powder
- 1/2 tsp sugar
- 1/2 tsp salt (i omit)
- 1/8 tsp pepper

Direction

- In skillet, brown steak in oil.
- Transfer to a 5-quart slow cooker
- In the same skillet, sauté onion for 1 minute
- Gradually add water, stirring to loosen browned bits from pan.
- Add remaining ingredients; bring to boil.
- Pour over flank steak.
- Cover and cook on low for 7-8 hours or until meat is tender. Slice the meat, serve with onion and pan juices.

104.   Slow Cooked Hungarian Goulash Recipe

Serving: 68 | Prep: | Cook: 480mins | Ready in:

Ingredients

- • 2 pounds round steak, cut into 1-inch cubes

- • 1 cup chopped onion
- • 2 tablespoons all-purpose flour
- • 1-1/2 teaspoons paprika
- • 1 teaspoon garlic salt
- • 1/2 teaspoon pepper
- • 1 can (14-1/2 ounces) diced tomatoes, undrained
- • 1 bay leaf
- • 1 cup (8 ounces) sour cream
- • Hot cooked noodles
- • Minced fresh parsley, optional

Direction

- Place beef and onion in a 3-qt. slow cooker.
- Combine the flour, paprika, garlic salt and pepper; sprinkle over beef and stir to coat.
- Stir in tomatoes.
- Add bay leaf.
- Cover and cook on low for 8-10 hours or until meat is tender.
- Discard bay leaf. Just before serving, stir in sour cream; heat through.
- Serve with noodles. Sprinkle with parsley if desired

105.   Slow Cooked Italian Pork Chops Recipe

Serving: 6 | Prep: | Cook: 360mins | Ready in:

Ingredients

- 6 boneless pork chops about 1/2" thick
- 1 jar (26 oz.) marinara sauce
- 1/2 pint fresh mushrooms, chopped
- 1 red bell pepper, chopped
- 1 chopped onion
- 3 cloves garlic, chopped
- 1 tsp. sugar
- 1 tsp. salt
- 1/2 tsp, black pepper
- 8 oz. mozzarella cheese, shredded

Direction

- Wash chops and pat dry with paper towels. Season with salt and pepper. Heat oil in skillet and fry chops brown on both sides. Put in crockpot. Top with vegetables. Mix marinara with sugar and a little more salt and pepper. Pour over vegetables; don't stir mix. Cover and cook on low 6 hours or until chops are tender. When ready to serve

---

106. Slow Cooked Lamb Chops Recipe

Serving: 4 | Prep: | Cook: 360mins | Ready in:

Ingredients

- 1 medium white onion sliced
- 1 teaspoon dried oregano
- 1/2 teaspoon dried thyme
- 1/2 teaspoon garlic powder
- 1/4 teaspoon salt
- 1/8 teaspoon ground black pepper
- 8 lamb loin chops
- 2 cloves garlic minced

Direction

- Place onion in a slow cooker.
- Combine oregano, thyme, garlic powder, salt and pepper then rub over lamb chops.
- Place chops over onion then top with garlic and cover then cook on low setting 6 hours.

---

107. Slow Cooked Pork Chops Recipe

Serving: 4 | Prep: | Cook: 420mins | Ready in:

Ingredients

- 6 to 8 boneless pork chops (about 2 1/2 pounds)
- 2 tablespoons oil
- salt and pepper
- 1 (10 3/4-ounce) can cream of mushroom soup
- 1 cup milk
- Hot cooked rice

Direction

- Brown pork chops in oil in frying pan over medium-high heat. Season with salt and pepper to taste. Transfer pork chops to slow cooker. Combine soup and milk. Pour over top. Cook at 225 degrees for 7 to 10 hours. Serve over rice.
- Variations: For added flavor, substitute garlic salt for salt.

---

108. Slow Cooked Sirloin Recipe

Serving: 6 | Prep: | Cook: 270mins | Ready in:

Ingredients

- 1 boneless beef sirloin steeak(1-1/2 lbs.)
- 1 medium onion,cut in 1" chunks
- 1 medium green pepper,cut in 1' chunks
- 1 can(14-1/2 oz) reduced- sodium beef broth
- 1/4 c worcestershire sauce
- 1/4 tsp dill weed
- 1/4 tsp dried thyme
- 1/4 tsp pepper
- Dash crushed red pepper flakes
- 2 Tbs cornstarch
- 2 Tbs water

Direction

- In large non-stick skillet coated with spray, brown beef on both sides. Place onion and green pepper in 3 qt. slow cooker. Top with beef. Combine broth, Worcestershire sauce, dill, thyme, pepper and pepper flakes; pour over beef. Cover and cook on high 3-4 hours or till meat reaches desired doneness and vegetables are crisp tender.

- Remove beef and keep warm. Combine cornstarch and water until smooth; gradually stir into cooking juices. Cover and cook about 30 mins longer or until slightly thickened. Return beef to cooker; heat through.

109. Slow Cooked Steak Rolls Recipe

Serving: 6 | Prep: | Cook: 480mins | Ready in:

Ingredients

- 1-1/2 pounds beef round steak 1/4" thick
- 1/2 teaspoon salt
- 1 teaspoon freshly ground black pepper
- 1/4 cup chopped white onion
- 2 tablespoons chopped parsley
- 1/2 teaspoon crushed dried basil
- 2 tablespoons flour
- oil
- 1 can cream of mushroom soup
- 1/4 cup catsup
- 1 teaspoon worcestershire sauce

Direction

- Trim fat and pound steak until very thin then cut into 8 equal pieces.
- Sprinkle with salt and pepper.
- Combine onion, parsley and basil then place equal amounts in middle of each meat piece.
- Roll up and tuck edges in around stuffing then tie or secure with toothpicks.
- Coat meat rolls with flour and brown in hot oil in skillet then drain and place in crock pot.
- Combine soup, catsup and Worcestershire sauce then pour over meat.
- Cook on low for 8 hours then remove toothpicks and serve with sauce.

110. Slow Cooker Barbacoa Shredded Beef Recipe

Serving: 6 | Prep: | Cook: 7mins | Ready in:

Ingredients

- 3 pound tri tip or chuck roast, some fat trimmed off(leave some for flavor) Cut into about 4 or 5 large pieces
- 1/2 a yellow onion quartered
- 2 large garlic cloves cut in quarters
- 1 jalapeno, chopped- stem and seeds removed if you dont want to spicy
- 2 tbs of chili powder
- 1/2 tsp of garlic powder
- 1/4 tsp onion powder
- 1/2 tsp pepper
- salt to taste, I add about 1 1/2 tsp salt
- 1 -2 cups of water

Direction

- Place all ingredients in slow cooker, and add enough water. Set on low and let cook for about 7-8 hours until very moist and shreds easily. There should be enough liquid to keep it moist; or cook on high for about 4-5 hours. Enjoy!

111. Slow Cooker Butterfly Chops And Potatoes Recipe

Serving: 6 | Prep: | Cook: 420mins | Ready in:

Ingredients

- 6 or more medium red potatoes, thickly sliced
- 1 large onion, quartered, thickly sliced
- 4 to 6 boneless butterflied pork chops
- 1 packet Zesty Italian dressing mix
- salt and pepper, to taste

Direction

- Toss potatoes and onion with salt and pepper; top with pork chops. Sprinkle chops with dressing mix. Cover and cook on LOW 7 to 9 hours. (A 4-1/2 quart or larger pot will be necessary for the larger number of chops and potatoes.)

---

112. Slow Cooker Hawaiian Beef Recipe

Serving: 5 | Prep: | Cook: 22mins | Ready in:

Ingredients

- 1/3 cup firmly packed brown sugar
- 1/3 cup cider vinegar
- 1 (8-ounce) can pineapple chucks, drained, erserve juice
- 3 tbs soy sauce
- 1 tps finely chopped freah garlic
- 2 tbs butter
- 1 1/2 pounds round steak, cut into 1 1/2-inch pieces
- 1 cup baby-cut carrots, halved crosswise
- 1 large onion, cutinto 1- inch pieces
- 3 tbs cornstarch
- 3 tbs cold water
- 1 large green bell pepper, cut into bite-size pieces
- Hot cooked rice
- green onion slices, if desired

Direction

- Combine brown sugar, vinegar, reserved pineapple juice, soy sauce and garlic in small bowl, stir until sugar is dissolved. Set aside.
- Melt 1 tbsp. butter in 12-inch skillet until sizzling, add half of steak pieces. Cook over med-high heat. Repeat with remaining butter and steak pieces.
- Add carrots and onion to slow cooker. Pour pineapple juice mixture over vegetables.

Cover, cook on Low heat setting for 7 to 9 hrs, or on High setting for 3 to 4 hrs or until meat is tender.
- Dissolve cornstarch in cold water in small bowl. Stir cornstarch mixture, pineapple chunks and green pepper into beef mixture. Cover, continue cooking 30 mins or until green pepper is crisply tender and juices are thickened. Serve over hot rice.

---

113. Slow Cooker Italian Pork Chops Recipe

Serving: 4 | Prep: | Cook: 480mins | Ready in:

Ingredients

- 4 thick, bone-in pork chops, at least 1 inch thick, blotted dry.
- 8oz mushrooms, sliced
- 1 medium onion, chopped
- 1 large yellow or red bell pepper, seeded and julienned
- 1 clove garlic, minced
- 2 (8oz) cans tomato sauce
- 2 T balsamic vinegar
- 2 T fresh flat-leaf parsley, minced
- 1/2 tsp dried oregano
- 1/2 tsp dried basil
- pinch of salt
- 2 T cornstarch
- 1/4 cup cold water

Direction

- Brown the pork chops on both sides.
- In the slow cooker, combine the mushrooms, onion, bell pepper, and garlic. Place the chops on top.
- In a bowl, combine the tomato sauce, vinegar, parsley, oregano, basil, and salt. Pour over the chops.
- Cover and cook on LOW until the meat is tender, 6 to 8 hours.

- Transfer the pork to a platter and tent with aluminum foil to keep warm.
- Transfer the tomato sauce to a saucepan. In a small bowl, whisk together the water and cornstarch until smooth, and stir into the sauce.
- Bring to a boil over medium heat, stirring until slightly thickened, about 2 minutes.

114. Slow Cooker Philly Style Cheese Steak Sandwiches Recipe

Serving: 6 | Prep: | Cook: 480mins | Ready in:

Ingredients

- 1 1/2 lbs beef round steak
- 1 medium green pepper, sliced thin
- 1 medium onion, sliced thin
- 1 (14 oz) can vegetable broth (can use beef - I've even used chicken in a pinc h)
- 1 envelope Italian dressing mix
- 1 large loaf French bread, siced into sandwich lengths
- 6 slices provolone cheese

Direction

- Spray crock pot with cooking spray
- Cut meat into strips, place in slow cooker
- Add green pepper, onion, broth, and dressing mix
- Cover and cook on low 7-8 hours, or high 3-4 hours
- Spoon meat mixture onto bread, top with a slice of cheese
- Another option is to toast bread in a 375 oven for 5-10 minutes, add meat, cover with cheese, then bake an additional 5 minutes to melt the cheese.

115. Slow Cooker Pork Chops Recipe

Serving: 0 | Prep: | Cook: 5hours4mins | Ready in:

Ingredients

- 6-8 thick pork chops (if you must use thin ones, reduce crock pot time by an hour and a half)
- 1 can (14 or 15 ounces) chicken or vegetable broth
- 1/4 cup brown sugar (not packed)
- 1/2 teaspoon ginger
- 1/4 teaspoon seasoned salt
- 1/4 teaspoon garlic powder
- 1/4 cup ketchup
- flour or cornstarch (optional)

Direction

- Mix all ingredients except pork chops together in a bowl.
- Place pork chops on bottom of crock pot.
- Pour mixture over chops.
- Cook on low 4-5 hours or until pork is tender.
- If using the leftover liquid as a gravy, add a little bit of flour or cornstarch to thicken.

116. Slow Cooker Pork Colorado Recipe

Serving: 8 | Prep: | Cook: 8hours20mins | Ready in:

Ingredients

- 1 large pork tenderloin
- 1 cup olive oil
- 2 Tsp horseradish
- 5 cloves garlic, minced
- 1 cup beer
- 1 tsp dry mustard
- 1/2 cup soy sauce
- 2 tsp. brown sugar
- 3 tbsp. worcestershire sauce

- 1 tsp salt
- 2 tsp white pepper

Direction

- Combine all ingredients and place in crockpot on medium too high for 8 hours. That it!

---

117.   Slow Cooker Smothered Round Steak Recipe

Serving: 6 | Prep: | Cook: 8hours7mins | Ready in:

Ingredients

- 3lbs Bottom round steaks
- 1 can great northern beans(or other white bean), undrained
- 1 can Italain style diced tomatoes
- 8oz fresh baby spinach(no need to chop)
- 1 medium onion, chopped
- 4 cloves garlic, minced
- 1T worcestershire sauce
- 1 lime or 1/2 lemon
- kosher or sea salt and fresh ground black pepper(or your favorite salt blend and black pepper)

Direction

- Spray slow cooker bowl with no stick spray. Place steaks in bottom of slow cooker.
- Sprinkle with salt/pepper or seasoned salt and lime or lemon juice.
- Add entire can of tomatoes, onion, garlic and Worcestershire sauce.
- Cook on low for about 4 hours.
- Add beans, taste broth and re-season.
- Cook another 2-4 hours until meat is tender. Meat will remain "tough" then all the sudden, it will just fall apart (mine took 7 hours).
- Add spinach, return lid to pot, lower to warm or turn off, and let rest while preparing rest of meal. This should be enough time to heat and

wilt the spinach...you don't want it over cooked.
- Serve by removing each steak and spooning the veggie mixture over meat with a slotted spoon. This will yield a LOT of liquid even though very little is added.

---

118.   Slow Cooker Spicy Pork And Cabbage Recipe

Serving: 2 | Prep: | Cook: 300mins | Ready in:

Ingredients

- 4 to 6 pork loin chops, trimmed, 1-inch thick
- salt and pepper, to taste
- Kitchen Bouquet
- 4 cups coarsely shredded cabbage
- 3 or 4 tart apples, cored and diced
- 1/2 small onion, chopped
- 2 whole cloves
- 1/2 small bay leaf
- 1-3/8 cups sugar
- 1 cup water
- 2 tablespoons cider vinegar
- 2 teaspoons salt

Direction

- Season pork chops lightly with salt and pepper; and brush with Kitchen Bouquet. Set aside.
- Place cabbage, apples and onion in a crockpot. Add remaining ingredients, except pork chops. Toss together well to evenly distribute spices. Arrange chops on top of cabbage mixture; stacking to fit.
- Cover and cook on LOW for 8 to 10 hours, or on HIGH for 4 to 5 hours.

119.   Slow Cooker Sweet Sour Chicken Recipe

Serving: 6 | Prep: | Cook: 315mins | Ready in:

Ingredients

- 1 1/2 lb. boneless skinless chicken cut into 1" pieces (or pork)
- 1 medium onion, chopped
- 3/4 C. sliced carrots
- 1 14oz. can chicken broth
- 1 tbsp. soy sauce (optional)
- 1 14oz. bottle Kraft sweet&sour sauce
- 1/4 tsp. black pepper
- 1 14oz. can pineapple chunks, drained
- 1 medium green pepper chopped
- 2 cups Minute Rice uncooked

Direction

- Place chicken in slow cooker, top with onion, carrots, broth, pepper, and sauces. Put on lid.
- Cook on low 8 hrs. Or high for 5 hrs.
- Add pineapple, green pepper, and rice. Cook an additional 30 minutes. (I usually add the green peppers half way thru as I don't like them crunchy)

120.   Slow Cooked Cherry Pork Chops Recipe

Serving: 6 | Prep: | Cook: 240mins | Ready in:

Ingredients

- 6 bone-in pork loin chops(3/4" thick)
- 1/8tsp salt
- dash of pepper
- 1c canned cherry pie filling
- 2tsp lemon juice
- 1/2tsp chicken bouillon granules
- 1/8 tsp ground mace

Direction

- In a skillet coated with non-stick cooking spray, brown the pork chops over medium heat on both sides. Season with salt and pepper.
- In a slow cooker, combine pie filling, lemon juice, bouillon and mace. Add pork chops. Cover and cook on low for 3-4 hours or until meat is no longer pink.

121.   Slow Cooked Elk Pepper Steak Recipe Recipe

Serving: 6 | Prep: | Cook: 3mins | Ready in:

Ingredients

- 2 lbs elk round steak
- 1/4 cup soy sauce
- 1 cup chopped onion
- 1 tablespoon chopped garlic
- 1 teaspoon sugar
- 1/2 tsp. salt
- 1/4 teaspoon pepper
- 1/4 teaspoon ginger
- 1 can stewed tomatoes
- 2 large green pepper cut into strips
- 1/2 cup cold water
- 11/2 tablespoons cornstarch
- cooked noodles or rice

Direction

- Cut elk round steak into strips. Mix next nine ingredients in slow cooker. Add elk meat. Cook on low for 8 to 10 hrs. Combine the cold water and cornstarch; add to crockpot, cook until thickened, about 15 more minutes. Serve over noodles or rice.

122. Slow Cooked Pepper Steak Recipe

Serving: 68 | Prep: | Cook: 360mins | Ready in:

Ingredients

- 1 1/2 - 2 lbs. beef round steak
- 2 Tbsp. cooking oil
- 1/4 cup soy sauce
- 1/2 cup chopped onion
- 1 clove garlic, minced
- 1 tsp. sugar
- 1/2 tsp. salt
- 1/4 tsp. pepper
- 1/4 tsp. ground ginger
- 4 tomatoes, cut into eighths
- 2 large green peppers, sliced into strips
- 1/2 cup cold water
- 1 Tbsp. cornstarch
- rice or noodles

Direction

- Cut beef into 3 x 1-in. strips; brown in oil
- Transfer to slow cooker.
- Combine next 7 ingredients; pour over beef.
- Cover and cook on low 5-6 hours.
- Add tomatoes and green pepper.
- Cook on low 1 hour longer.
- Make paste out of water and cornstarch.
- Stir into liquid in slow cooker and cook on high until thickened.
- Serve over rice or noodles.

123. Slow Cooked Pork Chops Supreme Recipe

Serving: 4 | Prep: | Cook: 480mins | Ready in:

Ingredients

- 1 onion, sliced thin
- 1 large potato, peeled and chunked
- 1 can cream of chicken soup
- 4 pork chops, trimmed of fat
- salt and pepper to taste
- Sprinkle to taste with garlic powder or adobo seasoning

Direction

- 1. Place onions and potatoes in bottom of crockpot. Lightly sprinkle with salt.
- 2. Top with pork chops. Season lightly with salt and pepper. Sprinkle some garlic powder over it. Pour soup over top. Cover; cook on low for 8 hours or on high for 4-5 hours.

124. Smoked Pork Chops & Sauerkraut Recipe

Serving: 6 | Prep: | Cook: 480mins | Ready in:

Ingredients

- 2 lbs smoked pork chops
- 1 bag (2 lb) sauerkraut, rinsed and drained
- 3/4 lb small red potatoes
- 1 c fruity red wine
- 1/2 c baby carrots
- 1/2 c chopped onion
- 1 tsp ground black pepper
- 1 tsp dried thyme

Direction

- Coat 4 qt. or larger slow cooker with cooking spray.
- Cut pork chops, if necessary, into pieces that fit into cooker. Add pork, sauerkraut, potatoes, wine, carrots, onion, pepper, and thyme into cooker.
- Cover. Cook on low 8 to 9 hours or high 4 to 4-1/2 hours.

125.   Sour Cream Pork Chops Recipe

Serving: 5 | Prep: | Cook: 7mins | Ready in:

Ingredients

- 5 pork chops
- salt and pepper to taste
- garlic powder to taste
- 1/c flour
- 1 lg. onion, sliced 1/4"thick
- 2 cubes chicken bouillon
- 2c boiling water
- 2Tbs flour
- 1(8oz) container sour cream

Direction

- Season chops with salt, pepper and garlic powder, then dredge in flour. In skillet, over med. heat, lightly brown chops in small amt. of oil; place in slow cooker and top with onion slices.
- Dissolve bouillon in boiling water and pour over chops. Cook on low for 7 to 8 hours.
- After chops have cooked, remove from slow cooker and keep warm. Be careful, chops are so tender they will fall apart. In bowl, blend 2Tbs. flour with sour cream; mix into meat juices. Turn slow-cooker to high for 15 to 30 mins until sauce is slightly thickened. Serve sauce over chops.

126.   Southwestern Flank Steak With Black Beans Recipe

Serving: 8 | Prep: | Cook: 6mins | Ready in:

Ingredients

- 1 ½ lbs. flank steak
- 1 onion, chopped
- 3 cloves garlic, minced
- 16 oz. jar chunky salsa
- ½ teaspoon dried oregano leaves
- 2 teaspoons chili powder
- ½ teaspoon salt
- ¼ teaspoon pepper
- 15 oz. can black beans, drained and rinsed
- 1 can shoepeg corn
- 1 red bell pepper, sliced
- 1 yellow bell pepper, sliced
- 3 cups hot cooked rice
- Shredded Monterrey Jack or pepper Jack cheese
- Chopped Fresh cilantro

Direction

- Trim excess fat from steak.
- Place onions, peppers and garlic in bottom of 3-4 quart slow cooker and top with steak.
- Mix salsa, oregano, chili powder, salt, and pepper in small bowl and pour over meat.
- Top with drained black beans and corn.
- Cover and cook on low 6-8 hours until steak is cooked through and vegetables are tender.
- Serve over cooked rice
- Top with shredded cheese and chopped cilantro

127.   Spicy Pork Chops With Black Eyed Peas Recipe

Serving: 4 | Prep: | Cook: 9hours15mins | Ready in:

Ingredients

- 8 pork chops, thick
- 30 ounces black-eyed peas, canned
- 1 can beef broth
- 2 cubes beef bouillon
- 1 medium onion, chopped
- 1 teaspoon salt
- 1/4 teaspoon freshly ground black pepper
- 1/4 small can jalapeno peppers (adjust to taste)

Direction

- Trim the fat from the pork chops and use it to grease a large skillet.
- Over high heat, brown each chop on both sides. As each chop is finished, season with salt and pepper before placing in the stoneware.
- Scrape the pan juices and turn them into the stoneware.
- Add chopped onion, beef broth and beef cubes. Cover and cook on low for about 7 hours.
- Add black-eyed peas with juice, cover and cook for an additional 2 hours on low.

128. Squash And Pork Chops In The Crockpot Recipe

Serving: 6 | Prep: | Cook: 480mins | Ready in:

Ingredients

- 6 thick pork chops
- 2 medium acorn squash
- 3/4 teaspoon salt
- 2 tablespoons margarine melted
- 3/4 cup brown sugar
- 3/4 teaspoon browning sauce
- 1 tablespoon orange juice
- 1/2 teaspoon orange peel grated

Direction

- Trim excess fat from pork chops.
- Cut each squash into 5 crossway slices then remove seeds.
- Arrange 3 chops on bottom of crackpot.
- Place all squash slices on top then another layer of three remaining chops.
- Combine salt, butter, sugar, sauce, juice and peel then spoon over chops.
- Cover and cook on low for 8 hours.
- Serve one or two slices of squash with each pork chop

129. Steak N Gravy Recipe

Serving: 6 | Prep: | Cook: 120mins | Ready in:

Ingredients

- Package round steak
- 1/4 onion finely diced
- 3 cups water
- 5 or 5 beef boulion cubes
- pepper to taste

Direction

- Cut round steak into serving size pieces. Add to crock pot with rest of the ingredients. Cook 4-6 hours on low. When steak is done cooking, add a 3/4 c water mixed with 1/2 c flour that has been well mixed to crock pot. Stir well. Cook another 10-15 minutes. Serve over rice or with mashed potatoes.

130. Stuffed Baby Zucchini And Vine Leaves With Lamb Chops Recipe

Serving: 10 | Prep: | Cook: 2mins | Ready in:

Ingredients

- 18 pieces or 1500g small size baby zucchini
- 35 medium size vine leaves
- 1 ¼ or 250g Egyptian rice, soaked in water for 1 hour and drained
- 500g lamb meat, minced
- 1 medium or 150g tomato, chopped
- 4 tablespoons unsalted butter, melted
- ¼ cup or 60ml water
- 1 ¼ teaspoon salt
- 1 tablespoon cinnamon powder
- ½ teaspoon ground black pepper
- 1 teaspoon mixed spices, ground(cumin,bay leaves,zaffaran,turmeric)

- 1 small pinch ground nutmeg
- 1 tablespoon vegetable oil
- 1 kg lamb chops, cleaned from fat
- 4 cubes mutton stock
- 8 cloves garlic, peeled
- Additional 10 cups or 2 ½ liters water
- ½ cup or 125ml lemon juice
- 1 tbs ground dry mint
- 5 tbs tomato paste

Direction

- Hollow baby zucchini and then remove extra stems from the vine leaves. Wash both well, drain and set them aside.
- In a bowl, combine and mix rice, minced lamb, tomato, butter, water, salt and spices and set in fridge for ½ hour.
- Stuff baby zucchini with this mixture and keep 1cm empty from the top and set aside.
- To stuff a vine leaves; place it on a working board with the dull side and the stem facing up. Place a teaspoon of the stuffing on the lower part of the leaves, fold the outside edges towards the centre and roll tightly into the shape of a finger.
- Heat the oil in large pot and fry lamb chops for 5 minutes or until brown in colour. Remove pot from heat. Arrange lamb chops evenly then add the whole peeled garlic, crumble Mutton Stock cubes over the lamb chops.
- Lines with 1 layer of unstuffed leaves over the lamb chops then place the rolled stuffed leaves above them alternating the direction of each layer.
- Place stuffed baby zucchini over the stuffed vine leaves side by side.
- Secure zucchinis with a plate on top.
- Add the tomato paste to the water and stir till it dissolve completely
- Add the water to the zucchini and bring to boil (add salt to your taste) then simmer on low heat for 2 hours or until baby zucchini is well cooked.
- Add lemon juice and dry mint.
- Boil for more 5 minutes
- Remove from heat.

- Add more hot water if it's needed during boiling to make sure zucchini is covered with water.
- To serve:
- Place the vine leaves in the middle of a round plate, the zucchini around them and put the lamb chops over the vine leaves.
- Put the sauce in a separate saucer.
- Note: When the food is well cooked, uncover and leave for few minutes to rest, then serve the vine leaves and the zucchini.

131.   Stuffed DILLicious Flank Steak Recipe

Serving: 8 | Prep: | Cook: 360mins | Ready in:

Ingredients

- 2 pounds flank steak (also known as London broil)
- 1 tbsp Montreal steak spice
- 1 cup chopped onion
- 3 tbsp minced garlic
- 1 cup fresh mushrooms- thinly sliced
- ¼ cup dried dill
- 1 (10.5 ounce) can onion soup- do not dilute

Direction

- Pound steak on both sides with a meat mallet to help tenderize the beef.
- Sprinkle with steak seasoning.
- Set aside.
- Mix onion, garlic, mushrooms, and dill together until well mixed. Spread on seasoned steak.
- Roll lengthwise (starting at the longest side of the steak) jellyroll style and tie with string about every 2-inches.
- Place in slow cooker.
- Pour onion soup into slow cooker.
- Cover. Cook on low for 6 hours

132.   Sweet And Sour Slow Cooker Flank Steak Recipe

Serving: 6 | Prep: | Cook: 240mins | Ready in:

Ingredients

- 2 large garlic cloves minced
- 9 ounces frozen chopped onions
- 16 ounces canned mushrooms sliced and well drained
- 24 ounces chili sauce
- 1/2 cup beef broth
- 2 tablespoons canned tomato paste
- 1/4 cup dry red wine
- 1 teaspoon salt
- 1 teaspoon paprika
- 1 teaspoon freshly ground black pepper
- 1 tablespoon balsamic vinegar
- 1 tablespoon unpacked brown sugar
- 3 pounds raw lean flank steak cut into six equal pieces

Direction

- Stir garlic, onion, mushrooms, sauce, broth, paste, wine, salt, paprika, pepper, vinegar and sugar.
- Place steak in slow cooker and pour garlic mixture over top then stir briefly.
- Cover cooker and cook on high 4 hours then remove steak and let sit 2 minutes.
- Slice against the grain then arrange steak on a platter and spoon vegetables and gravy on top.

133.   Sweet Slow Cooker Pork Chops Recipe

Serving: 4 | Prep: | Cook: 480mins | Ready in:

Ingredients

- 6 bone-in pork loin chops
- 1-16 ounce can jellied cranberry sauce
- 1/2 cup cranberry juice or apple juice
- 1/4 cup sugar
- 2 tablespoons spicy brown mustard
- 2 tablespoons cornstarch
- 1/4 cup water
- salt and pepper to taste
- mashed potatoes to serve with

Direction

- Place pork chops in slow cooker.
- Combine cranberry sauce, juice, sugar and mustard until smooth.
- Pour over pork chops.
- Cover and cook on low for 7-8 hours, or until meat is tender.
- Remove chops and keep them warm.
- In a saucepan, combine cornstarch with water until smooth.
- Gradually stir in cooking juices and bring to a boil.
- Cook and stir for about 3 minutes until thickened.
- Season with salt and pepper.
- Serve pork over mashed potatoes and pour over some gravy.

134.   Swiss Bernerplatte Recipe

Serving: 4 | Prep: | Cook: 480mins | Ready in:

Ingredients

- 1 lb. bag of refrigerator sauerkraut
- 1 large idaho potato, peeled and sliced
- 3 smoked pork chops
- 2 knockwurst sausages
- 1 link of Polish kielbasa
- salt and pepper (1/2 tsp of each)
- 1/2 tsp of caraway seeds
- 1 12 ounce can of amber bock beer

Direction

- Salt and pepper sliced potatoes and chops.
- Place in layers in the slow cooker pot:
- Sauerkraut, potatoes, sauerkraut, pork chops, sauerkraut, knockwurst, sauerkraut, kielbasa.
- Sprinkle with caraway.
- Pour the beer over all.
- Cook on low for 8 hours.
- Serve with mustard, bread and butter.

135.   Swiss Steak Stew Recipe

Serving: 6 | Prep: | Cook: 78mins | Ready in:

Ingredients

- 1/4 cup all-purpose flour
- 1/2 teaspoon salt
- 1 1/2 pounds boneless round steak, cut into bite size pieces
- 1 (14.5 ounce) can Italian-style diced tomatoes
- 3/4 cup water or beef broth
- 3 cups peeled and quartered new red potatoes
- 1 onion, diced
- 1 cup frozen or can corn
- 1 cup frozen or can green beans
- 1 garlic bulb minced
- 1 cup carrots sliced
- 2 to 3 bay leaves
- pepper to taste

Direction

- In medium bowl, combine flour and salt; mix well. Add beef and coat well.
- Coat a nonstick skillet with cooking spray and heat over medium heat. Add beef and cook until browned.
- In a slow cooker, layer potatoes, beef and onion and carrots. Stir tomatoes with juice, water and any remaining flour mixture together. Pour over top. Cover and cook on low setting for 7 to 8 hours or until beef is tender. Add green beans and corn and cook for about 10 to 15 minutes; cook till warm.

136.   Swiss Steak WEgg Noodles Recipe

Serving: 6 | Prep: | Cook: 60mins | Ready in:

Ingredients

- round steak (trim excess fat)
- 1 Can Italian stewed tomatoes
- 1 small can tomato sauce
- olive oil
- McCormick swiss steak seasoning (I have bought the seasoning that comes with the bag and just saved the bag for another time!)
- 1 small onion cut into thin strips
- 1 green pepper sut into thins strips
- 1 pkg egg noodles
- 2 Tbsp butter

Direction

- Cut steak into large pieces
- Cover bottom of large skillet with Olive Oil
- Add steak to skillet so it covers the bottom
- Add onion & green pepper
- Cover steak & veggies with stewed tomatoes & sauce
- Bring to a boil, reduce heat, cover and simmer on Low for about 1 hour. I will turn the steak twice during this time.
- Boil Egg noodles
- Drain and add butter till melted
- Serve Swiss steak over noodles

137.   Swiss Steak With Round Steak And Tomatos Recipe

Serving: 46 | Prep: | Cook: 79mins | Ready in:

Ingredients

- 1 large cooking bag

- 1-2 pounds round steak 1/2 thick cut into sevreing size portions
- 2 tbsp. flour
- 2 cans(14.5 ounce each) diced tomatos
- 1 tsp. celery seed
- 2 tbsp. tomato paste
- 1 tbsp. prepared mustard
- 1 tbsp. worcestershire sauce
- 1 tbsp. brown sugar
- 3 ribs celery, thinly sliced
- 2 carrots, sliced 1/4 inch thick
- 1 small onion, chopped

Direction

- Add flour, tomatoes, celery seed, tomato paste, mustard, Worcestershire sauce, and brown sugar to cooking bag
- Squeeze bag to mix all ingredients
- Add vegetables and round steak to cooking bag.
- Secure top of bag with a tie and place in slow cooker
- Cut several small holes in the top of the bag to allow steam to escape
- Cover and cook in slow cooker on low for 7-9 hours
- Serve with mashed potatoes and green beans

138.   Swiss Steak Recipe

Serving: 5 | Prep: | Cook: 212mins |Ready in:

Ingredients

- 1 onion sliced and halved.
- 1 tbsp. vegetable oil.
- 1 electric skillet sized round steak, cubed.
- 2 cups water or to cover.
- 2 beef boulion cubes.
- 1 tbsp. multipurpose flour.
- 2pkgs. brown or mushroom gravy.
- 2 cans 15 ounce whole potatoes.
- salt and pepper to taste.

Direction

- Peel, half and slice onion.
- Preheat electric skillet to 350degrees.
- Add vegetable oil and onions.
- Cook about 5 minutes.
- Lightly flour round steak and shake off access.
- Add round steak to pan and cover with water.
- Bring to boil and reduce heat to 250 degrees.
- Add bouillon cubes and sprinkle with 1 tbsp. flour.
- Add 2 pkgs mushroom gravy and stir.
- Simmer covered on 200 degrees or low for about 2 hours.
- Turn round steak after about 1hour.
- Add potatoes, drained, at this time and continue to cook, covered for another 30 minutes.
- When meat is fork tender, remove and serve!

139.   Tangy Italian Beef Sandwiches Recipe

Serving: 12 | Prep: | Cook: 480mins |Ready in:

Ingredients

- 1 Bonless beef sirloin tip roast (3-4 lbs)
- 1/4 C Packed brown sugar
- 16 oz Bottle Italian dressing
- 2 t italian seasoning

Direction

- Spray inside of 3-4 quart slow cooker with cooking spray
- Place beef in cooker
- Sprinkle with brown sugar
- Pour dressing over beef
- Cover and cook on low 10-12 hours (I put it in before I go to bed and let it cook all night) or on high 6-8 hours
- Shred beef using two forks.
- Add Italian Seasoning and mix well

- Using slotted spoon to remove beef from cooker, fill buns with about 1/3 C of beef and serve with remaining juices to dip.
- ENJOY!

140.   Tender Crock Pot Boneless Pork Chops Recipe

Serving: 4 | Prep: | Cook: 6mins | Ready in:

Ingredients

- 4 boneless pork chops (othe meat works well too)
- favorite meat seasoning
- 1 can Dr. pepper
- 1 cup BBQ Sauce

Direction

- Put Dr. Pepper and BBQ sauce in the bottom of the crock pot.
- Add pork chops (or meat of choice- beef, chicken etc.)That have been sprinkled with seasoning
- Cook on high for 5-6 hours.

141.   Texas Beef Barbecue Recipe

Serving: 16 | Prep: | Cook: 480mins | Ready in:

Ingredients

- 1 boneless beef sirloin tip roast (4 pounds)
- 1 can (5-1/2 ounces) spicy hot V8 juice
- 1/2 cup water
- 1/4 cup white vinegar
- 1/4 cup ketchup
- 2 tablespoons worcestershire sauce
- 1/2 cup packed brown sugar
- 1 teaspoon salt

- 1 teaspoon ground mustard
- 1 teaspoon paprika
- 1/4 teaspoon chili powder
- 1/8 teaspoon pepper
- 16 kaiser rolls, split

Direction

- Cut roast in half; place in a 5-qt. slow cooker. Combine the V8 juice, water, vinegar, ketchup, Worcestershire sauce, brown sugar and seasonings; pour over roast. Cover and cook on low for 8-10 hours or until meat is tender.
- Remove meat and shred with two forks; return to slow cooker and heat through. Spoon 1/2 cup meat mixture onto each roll.

142.   Tri Tip And Wine Recipe

Serving: 8 | Prep: | Cook: 480mins | Ready in:

Ingredients

- 4 lb tri-tip roast (you can use any type of your favorite roast if you'd like, also feel free to go bigger or smaller on the size of the roast to work for your family)
- one packet onion soup mix
- 2 cups red wine (use whatever you have on hand, merlot seem to work the best though for my experimentation)

Direction

- Trim the roast of any large areas of fat, leave a little though, this really adds to the flavor
- Place roast in crock pot
- Sprinkle onion soup mix over roast
- Pour wine over roast
- Let cook 8 hours on low heat
- Eat and enjoy!!!
- PS- This makes great leftovers for sandwiches!!! If you're lucky enough to have any leftovers. My family and friends devour it!!!

143.   Wacky Ingredients But Oh So Good Pork Chops With Savory And Tangy Gravy Recipe

Serving: 4 | Prep: | Cook: 60mins | Ready in:

Ingredients

- 4 pork chops (1 or more per person depending upon hunger-meter and size of pork chop)(Can be bone in, or boneless pork chops)
- kosher salt and Fresh Cracked ground pepper
- 3/4 cup flour
- For Sauce: here goes anything wacky in your fridge
- 5 tablespoons ketchup
- 5 tablespoons grape jelly (yes jelly - can be strawberry or any jelly you have in fridge)
- 3 tablespoons low sodium soy sauce
- 3 tablespoons mustard
- 1 tablespoon dry mustard
- 2 tablespoons worcestershire sauce
- 3 fresh garlic cloves minced
- 2 tablespoon herbes de Province
- (if you don't have herbs de province then add 1/2 teaspoon dried time, 1/2 teaspoon dried tarragon, 1/4 teaspoon rosemary and up your pepper)
- 1/2 to 1 cup water
- 1/2 cup red wine (optional)
- 2 tablespoons olive oil & 1 tablespoon butter
- Equipment needed: Deep skillet with lid, 2 bowls: one for sauce and one for mixing up season flour.

Direction

- Take pork chops out of fridge, let come to room temperature and sprinkle generously on both sides with salt and ground pepper - set aside for now.
- Take one bowl, add dry mustard and a dash of salt and pepper to 3/4 cup of flour and mix till

incorporated. This is to be used to dredge your pork chops in.
- With other bowl, add ketchup, grape jelly, soy sauce, wet mustard, Worcestershire sauce, minced garlic and all herbs as listed.
- Add 1/2 cup water to sauce and mix till blended well. It maybe that some of the jelly didn't break down - that's ok, it will while cooking.
- Grab the heavy-duty skillet of yours, turn on the heat to a medium-high beneath the skillet and let get quite hot.
- While skillet is getting hot, grab those pork chops and dredge in seasoned flour, shake off excess.
- Put olive oil in skillet first, then add butter. If pan is ready, place pork chops into skillet.
- Do not move, (no, not you, the pork chops of course, let them get caramelized on one side - it may take up to five minutes)
- Turn pork chops over and let them brown for three minutes.
- Take 1/2 cup of wine and carefully pour into skillet to deglaze. If not using the red wine (or instead simply drinking it, just skip this step and go to next - no one will know)
- Then add sauce from bowl directly into skillet, turn down the heat from under skillet to be on low heat and let simmer at least 45 minutes
- Put lid on skillet while your dish simmers. This dish only gets better as the more time you simmer the dish, the tenderer your pork will be. I usually let it simmer for 1.5 hours.
- When ready, serve over egg noodles (1st choice) or penne (2nd choice) or rice. Reserve sauce for when you may reheat dish for the next day - delicious!

144.   Winning Round Steak Recipe

Serving: 46 | Prep: | Cook: 8mins | Ready in:

Ingredients

- round steak
- golden mushroom soup (I use 3, but I like it saucey)
- canned mushrooms (2 cans)
- salt
- pepper

Direction

- Brown round steak
- Cut into serving size pieces
- Put in crock pot
- Add canned mushrooms
- Add golden mushroom soup
- Cook in crock pot for 8 hrs.

145.   Camp Chili Recipe

Serving: 10 | Prep: | Cook: 60mins |Ready in:

Ingredients

- 2lb. ground round or steak cut into 1/2 in. cubes
- 1 large onion chopped
- 5 cloves garlic minced
- 3 28 oz.cans tomatoes with juice
- 2 medium green peppers cut large
- 1/2 lb. fresh mushrooms
- 1/4 cup chili powder
- 1 and a 1/2 tsp salt
- 1 tsp sugar
- 1 and 1/2tsp black pepper
- 1 and 1/2 tsp cayenne pepper
- 2 1lb cans pinto beans

Direction

- Brown meat and drain.
- Combine all ingredients; simmer, 45 min to 1 hour or until none.

146.   Crock Pot Italian Beef And Barley Soup Recipe

Serving: 6 | Prep: | Cook: 9mins |Ready in:

Ingredients

- 1 boneless beef top sirloin steak (about 1 1/2 pounds)
- 1 TBS vegetable oil
- 4 medium carrots or parsnips, sliced 1/4 inch thick
- 1 cup chopped onion
- 1 tsp dried thyme leaves
- 1/2 tsp dried rosemary
- 1/4 tsp black pepper
- 1/3 cup pearl barley
- 2 cans (141/2 ounces each) beef broth
- 1 can (141/2 ounces) diced tomatoes with italian seasoning, undrained

Direction

- 1. Cut beef into 1-inch pieces. Heat oil over medium-high heat in large skillet; brown beef on all sides. Set aside
- 2. Place carrots and onion in the CROCK-POT slow cooker; sprinkle with thyme, rosemary and pepper. Top with barley and meat.   Pour broth and tomatoes with juice over met. Cover, cook on low for 8 to 10 hours or on HIGH for 3 to 4 hours or until beef is tender.

147.   Crockpot Italian Beef Recipe

Serving: 8 | Prep: | Cook: 10mins |Ready in:

Ingredients

- beef roast (i use sirloin roast) about 3 to 4 lbs (i think this is right, i just grab what looks good)
- 1 medium jar of medium to hot giardiana (sp??) i used medium
- 1 can of low sodium beef broth

- crusty rolls
- provelone cheese

Direction

- Brown the beef; roast on all sides in a heavy skillet with a little oil.
- Place in crockpot.
- Dump in medium jar of giardana sp??
- Dump in can of low sodium beef broth.
- Cook on low for 10 hrs. or so until beef falls apart when forked.
- Shred beef into the juice in the crock pot.
- Turn on oven broiler.
- Open crusty roll; with tongs, place beef into the roll, top with a little extra giardana and top with slice of provolone cheese. Broil until cheese is melted. I then put a little juice onto the sandwich and enjoy...
- Very simple, delicious...

148.   Slow Cooker Fall Pork Chops Recipe

Serving: 6 | Prep: | Cook: 360mins | Ready in:

Ingredients

- 6 thick pork chops
- 2 medium acorn squash
- 2 Tbs. butter
- 3/4 tsp. Kitchen Bouquet
- 1 Tbs. orange juice
- 1/2 tsp. orange zest

Direction

- Trim excess fat from chops
- Cut each squash into 4-5 crossways slices
- Arrange 3 chops on bottom of crockpot
- Place all squash slices on top
- Layer last 3 chops on squash
- Combine rest of ingredients and spoon over chops

- Cover and cook on low 6-8 hours (when tender)
- Serve 2 slices of squash on each chop

149.   Smothered Steak Recipe

Serving: 6 | Prep: | Cook: 480mins | Ready in:

Ingredients

- 1 and 1/2 pounds chuck or round steak cut into strips
- 1/ 3 cup flour
- 1/2 teaspoon salt
- 1/4 teaspoon pepper
- 1 large onion sliced
- 2 bell peppers sliced any color
- 14 and 1/2 oz can stewed tomatoes
- 4 oz can mushrooms drained
- 2 tablespoons soy sauce
- 10 oz package frozen french cut green beans

Direction

- Layer steak in bottom of slow cooker.
- Sprinkle with flour, salt, and pepper stirring gently to coat the steak.
- Add remaining ingredients and stir gently to mix.
- Cover and cook on low setting for 8 hours.
- Serve with rice or mashed potatoes.

150.   Tender Beer Chops Recipe

Serving: 4 | Prep: | Cook: 420mins | Ready in:

Ingredients

- 4 pork chops-well trimmed
- 1 onion sliced
- 1 12ounce can or bottle of beer

- 2 cubes of chicken buillon or 2 Tsp.instant buillon
- 2 cloves of garlec-minced

Direction

- Place onion slices on bottom of slow cooker
- Place chops on onions
- Sprinkle garlic over chops
- Stir beer and bouillon and pour over all
- Cook on low for 7-8 hours-until pork is very tender

Index

Conclusion

Thank you again for downloading this book!

I hope you enjoyed reading about my book!

If you enjoyed this book, please take the time to share your thoughts and post a review on Amazon. It'd be greatly appreciated!

Write me an honest review about the book – I truly value your opinion and thoughts and I will incorporate them into my next book, which is already underway.

Thank you!

If you have any questions, **feel free to contact at:** *author@ciderrecipes.com*

Stacey Doe

ciderrecipes.com

Made in the USA
Las Vegas, NV
06 January 2022